Better Homes and Gardens®

Easy
Skillet Meals

Do your skillet proud with golden-hued Lemon Chicken, a money's worth main dish that is especially good with rice, fresh-cooked broccoli, and sliced tomatoes. You'll enjoy making it from the recipe on page 40.

On the cover: *These easy-to-make Pineapple-Plum-Glazed Pork Chops are cooked in an electric skillet with soy sauce and ginger. The main dish cooks in less than 45 minutes. (See the recipe on page 16.)*

BETTER HOMES AND GARDENS BOOKS
Editorial Director: Don Dooley
Managing Editor: Malcolm E. Robinson   Art Director: John Berg
Asst. Managing Editor: Lawrence D. Clayton   Asst. Art Director: Randall Yontz
Food Editor: Nancy Morton
Senior Food Editor: Joyce Trollope
Associate Editors: Rosalie Riglin, Sharyl Heiken, Rosemary C. Hutchinson
Assistant Editors: Elizabeth Strait, Sandra Mapes,
Catherine Penney, Elizabeth Walter
Designers: Harijs Priekulis, Faith Berven

CONTENTS

Our seal assures you that every recipe in Easy Skillet Meals is endorsed by the Better Homes and Gardens Test Kitchen. Each recipe is tested for family appeal, practicality, and deliciousness.

KNOW YOUR SKILLETS

Never underestimate what your skillets can do for you. For example, do you take them for granted—only use them for frying? If so, it's time to take another look at these trusty helpers and match them up with the recipes and tips in this book. Before long, you'll find that besides a frying pan, you have a griddle, a steamer, a poacher, a panbroiler, a cooker for braising meats, and a mini oven. The electric skillets do all these jobs and are thermostatically controlled, too. Some also come with broiling units or warming trays.

The challenge in skillet cookery has always been to prevent foods from sticking to the pan. This applies equally to fried and braised dishes. Success lies both with controlling the heat and with the type of skillet used.

Skillets are designed so that foods cook by heat applied to the bottom of the pan. In days gone by, the erratic heat from an open fire or coal stove meant that plenty of fat or liquid was necessary to keep the food afloat. The heavy black skillets did their best to distribute the heat, but the food was apt to be fat-soaked or soggy by today's standards.

Today, skillets are prettier and more practical than those of yesteryear. Various materials, alone or in combination, do away with hot spots in the pan. Modern gas or electric ranges have adjustable heat settings, and there are convenient, thermostatically controlled electric skillets to ensure even cooking.

A boon to skillet cooking is the development of nonstick coatings such as Teflon. These coatings make it possible to cook food with little or no butter, margarine, oil, or shortening. When used, the fat's role is primarily for flavor or special browning rather than to prevent sticking. Nonstick coatings hold up best when wooden, nylon, or other special utensils without sharp edges are used for stirring and turning foods during cooking.

Frypans with tight-fitting covers keep the steam of braised dishes inside the pan so foods do not stick even when only a small amount of liquid is used. In addition, the range burner or electric skillet can be turned low so that the cooking process is a gentle one.

Beautiful skillets come in many materials, colors, finishes, sizes, and weights. Some are multipurpose pans, others have particular uses in preparing foods from other nations.

(1) and (5) are **cast iron.** *(1) has a colorful porcelain enamel finish, while (5) is a handy square shape. (4), (6), (10), and (13) are* **aluminum** *of different weights and colorful exterior finishes. Many styles are available with nonstick linings. (7) is also* **aluminum,** *but without the enamel finish on the outside. Its shape makes it useful for omelets and crepes. (8) is made of* **stainless steel,** *with a nonstick lining. Sometimes, stainless steel pans have a core of copper or aluminum to help distribute the heat. (9) is made of* **tin** *and* **copper.** *Like the blazer pan of a chafing dish, this small pan is used for tabletop cooking. (11), shown here on a separate, electrically heated base, is made of* **pyroceram.** *(12) is a buffet-style electric frypan with a nonstick lining.*

(2) and (3) are special skillets for foreign cookery. (2) is a Spanish paella pan with a porcelain finish. (3) is a Chinese wok.

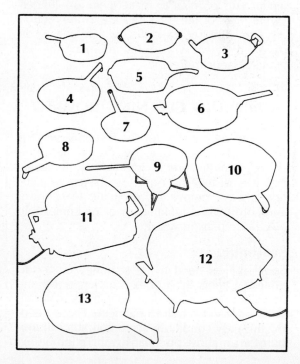

SPECIAL SKILLET USES

The pretty skillets available today are a far cry from those used a few generations ago. They equal their good looks in versatility, too.

Low-calorie cooking

Since not all skillet-cooked foods need to be fried, try poaching and panbroiling as two alternate cooking techniques. See pages 30-33 for specific ways to prepare satisfying main dishes that are low in calories.

Cost-cutting

Throughout the book all of the recipes that will help you to stretch the budget are flagged with a cost-cutting symbol.

Timesaving

The ability to cook foods quickly when necessary is one of the skillet's great advantages. The minutes trimmed from main dishes are particularly welcome. Be sure to try the Quick and Easy recipes that begin on page 10.

Meat-tenderizing

A skillet with a tight-fitting lid holds in the steam gathered during simmering or braising. The moisture softens connective tissue in less-tender cuts of meat to make them fork-tender. While most of these recipes are in the section on Time-Worthy Favorites, which begins on page 34, others will be found among the Regional American Recipes.

CARE AND CLEANING HOW-TO

Before using a skillet for the first time, wash it in hot sudsy water. Use your dishwasher if the skillet manufacturer's information indicates that it is dishwasher safe. As a safety precaution, always remove the automatic heat control and cord before dunking any of the immersible electric frypans in water.

Seasoning

Some skillets need to be seasoned or conditioned. Others have been seasoned by the manufacturer or are of a nonporous material, which doesn't require treatment. Those needing this easy conditioning are iron, some aluminum or an alloy, plus pans with Teflon lining.

To season cast iron and other porous metal skillets, lightly rub the inside of the clean, dry pan with cooking oil. Heat the pan in a 250° or 300° oven for several hours. Teflon-lined skillets do not need to be heated, but they should be rubbed with about a teaspoonful of cooking oil on a soft cloth or a paper towel. To retain this seasoning from one cooking time to the next, wash the skillet well after each use, but do not scour. When scouring is necessary, or after washing in an automatic dishwasher, reconditioning will be needed. (Care should be taken to use only plastic scouring pads on skillets with Teflon surfaces.)

Cleaning

The nonstick coating in your skillets may discolor after you have cooked in the pan for some time. Though unattractive, the discoloration does not affect cooking performance. Its cause is excessive heating of fat or food particles. Follow directions that came with the pan for removing it. A white film on the lining is merely an accumulation of minerals from the water. Wipe the film away with a cloth soaked in vinegar or lemon juice. Rinse, dry, and then recondition the surface.

A pan with an aluminum lining may also discolor through use. Clean it with a commercial cleaner, or boil 2 tablespoons cream of tartar in 2 quarts of water in the pan for 20 minutes. Rinse skillet well before using again.

The outside surfaces of porcelain skillets should be treated gently. Some will scratch with too vigorous an application of metal scouring pads or harsh cleansers. Soaking will usually remove burnt-on foods. Or, there are special cleansers available at the supermarket for this purpose. Several are formulated for cleaning the underside of electric skillets.

Never pour cold water in a hot skillet. Even though the pans have been well heat-tempered, the sudden change from very hot to very cold could cause the skillet to warp.

Storing

Ideally, skillets will be kept near the range, or if electric, near an outlet. Many styles are designed for hanging on the wall or on hooks inside a cabinet door. If a shelf or drawer is the best location, avoid stacking the pans, especially those with nonstick linings. Stacking can mar the finish.

ELECTRIC SKILLET KNOW-HOW

Begin your acquaintance with this versatile appliance by studying the use and care booklet. Once you know how to operate the skillet, you are ready to apply all the cooking techniques in the chart on this page and to follow the recipes in this cook book. Most recipes incorporate electric skillet temperatures in the recipe directions. The exceptions are those dishes involving amounts of food that are too small for such a large utensil.

The temperature control on the electric frypan is keyed to certain cooking operations, similar to those in the chart below. As you cook, you may find that you are choosing a slightly higher or lower setting. The variation is greatly influenced by the amount of food in the pan and by the setting at which water boils. The latter changes at different altitudes.

It is a good idea to take a few minutes and bring about 2 cups of water to boiling in your electric skillet. In this way you will know more accurately what setting is required to reach a full boil or to maintain a simmer.

Besides actually cooking in an electric skillet, foods such as frozen dinners or entrées can be warmed or heated. Preheat skillet with vent closed to 400° or 425°, as indicated on package. Then, place frozen meal on a rack in skillet; cover and heat for the specified time. Follow package directions if any part of the meal is to be opened partway through heating.

Electric frypan temperature guide

150° to 180° Warm
220° to 250° Simmer
250° to 275° Full Boil
275° to 300° Medium-low (to fry eggs)
300° to 350° Medium (to cook onion,
        celery, mushrooms,
        green pepper, etc.
        in butter or margarine)
350° to 400° High (to brown meat or
        to panbroil or panfry)
400° to 450° Hot (to keep temperature
        at 365° to 370° for
        shallow-fat frying)

Skillet glossary

Bake — To cook in a pan, an oven, or an oven-type appliance such as an electric skillet with tight-fitting cover.
Baste — To moisten foods during cooking with pan drippings or special sauce to add flavor and prevent drying.
Braise — To cook slowly with a small amount of liquid in a covered skillet.
Caramelize — To melt sugar slowly over low heat until it becomes brown.
Dry heat — To cook food, usually meat, in an uncovered pan and without the addition of liquid.
French fry — To cook by immersing food in hot fat at least 1½ inches deep.
Fry — To cook in hot shortening or oil.
Moist heat — To cook food, usually meat, in a tightly covered pan so that the steam held in the pan aids in cooking and tenderizing the meat.
Panbroil — To cook meat, uncovered, in a hot skillet, removing fat as it accumulates in the pan.
Panfry — To cook, uncovered, in a small amount of hot shortening or oil.
Poach — To cook in hot liquid, being careful that food retains its shape.
Pot roast — To braise a large cut of meat. The roast is usually browned well before the liquid is added.
Saute — To brown or cook in a small amount of butter or hot shortening.
Shallow-fat fry — To cook by immersing in the minimum depth of hot shortening or oil. (See tip, page 72.)
Simmer — To cook in liquid over low heat at a temperature where bubbles form at a slow rate and burst before reaching the surface. It is used frequently after the liquid has boiled rapidly and the heat is turned down for a long cooking period.
Steam — To cook in steam in a covered pan. A small amount of boiling water is used, more being added during cooking if necessary.
Stew — To simmer or braise slowly in a small amount of liquid.

Main Dishes

"What's for dinner?" is an old question. For a new answer, try serving one of these up-to-date skillet main dishes.

Recipes are divided according to the cooking time needed. All dishes in the Quick and Easy section are ready to serve in less than 1 hour. The Time-Worthy Favorites, as the name suggests, take longer.

Within the two sections the recipes are grouped by their principal ingredient — meat, poultry, seafood, or eggs. You will also find special groups of sandwiches, low-calorie dishes, and camping recipes.

Beef, especially ground beef, is a skillet standby, but flavorful pork, ham, lamb, and chicken are well represented. Although these skillet dishes were created with family meals in mind, many of them have company possibilities, too.

Delight the family soon with hearty *Skillet Hamburger Pie.* Cheese-topped potatoes wreathe this meat and vegetable one-dish meal. You'll find the recipe on page 13.

QUICK AND EASY DISHES

Call on your skillets to help you trim precious minutes from the time spent preparing lunch or dinner. Every main dish in this section cooks in 45 minutes or less—often much less. Wherever possible, preparation shortcuts are built into the recipe. Some convenience foods are used as ingredients, too. However, for all the emphasis on clock watching, no loss of flavor or attractiveness occurs in the foods.

You'll notice that some recipes are tagged with a cost-cutting symbol. This has been done so you can identify the dishes that are budget-stretching as well as delicious.

Meat Loaf in the Round

There's good mushroom cream gravy to serve with it—

      2 beef bouillon cubes
   1¼ cups boiling water
      1 beaten egg
   1½ cups soft bread crumbs
      ¼ cup chopped onion
      ½ teaspoon ground sage
      ¼ teaspoon salt
         Dash pepper
      1 pound ground beef
         Kitchen Bouquet
      1 3-ounce can sliced mushrooms
      1 tablespoon cornstarch
      ¼ cup dairy sour cream

Dissolve bouillon in the water; combine ¼ *cup* with egg, bread crumbs, onion, sage, salt, and pepper. Add ground beef; mix well. In 8-inch skillet shape mixture into circle slightly smaller than diameter of skillet. With handle of wooden spoon, make indentations in the meat to make 4 wedge-shaped pieces. Rub surface of meat with Kitchen Bouquet. Pour ½ *cup* of remaining bouillon around meat loaf; add mushrooms. Cook, covered, over low heat 25 to 30 minutes.

Transfer meat loaf to warm serving platter. Combine cornstarch and remaining bouillon; stir into pan juices. Cook and stir over low heat till thickened and bubbly. Stir in sour cream; heat through (do not boil). Makes 4 servings.

Cacciatore Sauce with Polenta

You can make the polenta the night before—

   3¾ cups water
      1 cup yellow cornmeal
      1 teaspoon salt
         • • •
      1 pound ground beef
      1 cup chopped onion
      1 6-ounce can sliced mushrooms, drained
      1 clove garlic, minced
      1 15-ounce can tomato sauce
      ½ cup water
      ¼ cup snipped parsley
      1 teaspoon dried sage leaves, crushed
      1 teaspoon shredded orange peel
      ½ teaspoon dried thyme leaves, crushed
         Grated Parmesan cheese

Polenta: In 10-inch skillet bring 2¾ cups of the water to a full, rolling boil. (Electric skillet 250°.) Combine remaining 1 cup water, cornmeal, and salt. Slowly stir into boiling water. Cook, stirring frequently, till thick, 10 to 15 minutes. Turn into 9-inch pie plate. Cover; chill till firm enough to cut, several hours or overnight.

Cacciatore Sauce: In 10-inch skillet cook ground beef, onion, mushrooms, and garlic till meat is browned and onion tender. (Electric skillet 350°.) Drain off excess fat. Add tomato sauce, water, parsley, sage, orange peel, and thyme. Cover and reduce heat (220°). Simmer 30 minutes. Cut polenta into 8 wedges. Press wedges down into sauce. Cover skillet and continue simmering till polenta is heated through, about 10 minutes. Serve sauce over polenta. Top with grated Parmesan cheese. Pass extra cheese. Makes 8 servings.

A skillet meal from northern Italy

When giblets from wild birds are cooked in an herb-seasoned tomato sauce, it's cacciatore or hunter-style sauce. Ground beef subs for giblets in this Cacciatore Sauce with Polenta (cornmeal mush) supper.

Frikadeller (Danish Meatballs)

1 pound lean ground beef
1 pound lean ground pork
¼ cup all-purpose flour
1 cup milk
2 eggs
1 teaspoon salt
¼ teaspoon ground allspice
¼ teaspoon ground nutmeg
   Cooking oil
1 cup water
2 tablespoons all-purpose flour
1 cup dairy sour cream

Beat meats, flour, milk, eggs, salt, allspice, and nutmeg till smooth. Drop meat mixture by table-spoons into lightly oiled skillet; flatten with spoon. Cook till lightly browned and cooked through, about 3 minutes per side. (Electric skillet 350°.) Repeat till all meat is cooked. Remove from skillet; keep warm.

Pour off excess fat. Stir water into pan drippings; bring to boil. Stir flour into sour cream. Stir small amount of the pan juices into sour cream; return to skillet. Cook and stir till thickened (do not boil). Add meatballs; heat through. Makes 6 to 8 servings.

Chili Mac

1 pound ground beef
1 cup chopped onion
¾ cup chopped green pepper
1 16-ounce can tomatoes, cut up
1 15-ounce can kidney beans, undrained
1 8-ounce can tomato sauce
½ cup water
2 teaspoons chili powder
1¼ teaspoons salt
1 bay leaf
1 cup uncooked elbow macaroni

In skillet cook meat, onion, and green pepper till meat is browned and vegetables are tender. (Electric skillet 350°.) Drain off fat. Stir in tomatoes, kidney beans, tomato sauce, water, chili powder, salt, and bay leaf. Bring to boiling; add macaroni. Cover and reduce heat (220°). Simmer, stirring frequently, till macaroni is cooked, 10 to 15 minutes. Remove the bay leaf before serving. Makes 6 servings.

Meatball Stew

1 beaten egg
1 10½-ounce can condensed
   cream of celery soup
1 cup soft bread crumbs
2 tablespoons dry onion soup mix
1 pound lean ground beef
2 tablespoons cooking oil
1 tablespoon all-purpose flour
½ teaspoon paprika
1 cup water
1 10-ounce package frozen mixed
   vegetables
1 small bay leaf
1 9-ounce package frozen crinkle-
   cut potatoes, French-fried

Combine egg, ¼ *cup* of celery soup, bread crumbs, and onion soup mix. Add beef; mix well. Shape into 16 meatballs; brown in 10-inch skillet in hot oil. (Electric skillet 350°.)

Blend remaining soup, flour, and paprika. Gradually add water. Pour mixture over meatballs. Rinse mixed vegetables quickly with hot water to separate pieces; drain. Add vegetables to skillet. Add bay leaf. Bring to boiling. Cover and reduce heat (220°). Simmer 20 minutes. Remove bay leaf. Add potatoes. Cover; simmer till potatoes are heated through, about 10 minutes. Makes 4 servings.

Sassy Zucchini

1 pound ground beef
1 cup chopped onion
¾ cup water
1 16-ounce can tomatoes, cut up
1 1-ounce envelope spaghetti sauce mix
1 teaspoon salt
1 cup uncooked packaged precooked rice
1½ pounds zucchini, cut in 1-inch strips
   (4 cups)

In large skillet cook ground beef and onion till meat is browned and onion is tender. (Electric skillet 350°.) Stir in water, *undrained* tomatoes, spaghetti sauce mix, and salt. Bring to boiling. Stir in rice and zucchini pieces. Cover tightly; reduce heat (220°). Simmer, stirring occasionally, till zucchini is tender, 15 to 20 minutes. Makes 6 servings.

Ground beef buying tips

● Choose ground beef to fit both recipe and budget. Remember that the leaner the ground beef, the more it costs. Use less expensive ground chuck or hamburger for saucy mixtures. Buy leaner ground round for meat loaves and for patties when cutting calories.

● Fresh ground beef packaged in plastic wrap at the meat case can be frozen without rewrapping for one or two weeks. However, for longer storage, wrap the meat in freezer material. Store frozen ground beef at 0°.

● Buy ground beef in bulk packages to save several cents per pound. At home, divide the meat into smaller units, wrap in freezer material and freeze.

Skillet Hamburger Pie

This recipe doubles easily in a buffet electric skillet, as pictured on page 8—

1½ pounds ground beef
½ cup coarsely chopped celery
½ cup chopped onion
 1 teaspoon Worcestershire sauce
¾ teaspoon salt
⅛ teaspoon pepper
 1 16-ounce can cut green beans, drained
 1 10¾-ounce can beef gravy
   Instant mashed potato buds
     (enough for 6 servings)
½ cup dairy sour cream
 1 tablespoon snipped chives
   Paprika
⅓ cup shredded process American cheese

In skillet cook beef, celery, and onion till meat is browned and vegetables crisp-tender. (Electric skillet 350°.) Stir in Worcestershire, ¼ *teaspoon* salt, pepper, beans, gravy, and ½ cup water. Reduce heat (220°); simmer to blend flavors. Whip potatoes and 2 cups boiling water; add sour cream, chives, and remaining salt. Spoon in mounds over meat. Top with paprika and cheese. Cover; heat till cheese melts. Serves 6.

Italian Skillet Meat Loaves

An easy-to-make main dish for two—

 1 beaten egg
¾ cup soft bread crumbs
⅓ cup milk
 2 teaspoons instant minced onion
 1 teaspoon dried parsley flakes
½ teaspoon garlic salt
   Dash pepper
½ pound lean ground beef
 2 3½x¾-inch sticks Monterey Jack cheese
 1 tablespoon cooking oil
 1 8-ounce can pizza sauce
   Hot cooked spaghetti

Combine egg, bread crumbs, milk, instant minced onion, parsley flakes, garlic salt, and pepper. Add ground beef; mix well. Divide mixture in half. Shape each portion into a little meat loaf around a stick of cheese. In a small skillet brown the loaves on all sides in hot oil. Pour off drippings. Add pizza sauce. Cover and reduce heat. Simmer 15 minutes. Serve with hot cooked spaghetti. Makes 2 servings.

Texas Beef Skillet

 1 pound lean ground beef
¾ cup chopped onion
1½ teaspoons chili powder
½ teaspoon salt
½ teaspoon garlic salt
 1 16-ounce can tomatoes, cut up
 1 15-ounce can red kidney beans,
     undrained
¾ cup uncooked packaged precooked rice
¾ cup water
 3 tablespoons chopped green pepper
¾ cup shredded sharp process American
     cheese (3 ounces)
   Corn chips, crushed

Brown the ground beef and onion in skillet over medium heat. (Electric skillet 350°.) Stir in chili powder, salt, garlic salt, tomatoes, beans, rice, water, and green pepper. Cover and reduce heat (220°). Simmer, stirring occasionally, 20 minutes. Top with cheese. Cover and heat till cheese melts, about 3 minutes. Sprinkle corn chips around the edge. Serves 6.

Give patties like Scallopini Burgers *a new dress by serving them over hot buttered noodles instead of spaghetti and by using ground veal rather than beef.*

Scallopini Burgers

1 beaten egg
2 tablespoons milk
1 cup soft bread crumbs
½ teaspoon salt
  Dash pepper
1½ pounds ground veal
¼ cup all-purpose flour
¼ cup cooking oil
1 8-ounce can tomato sauce (1 cup)
1 3-ounce can chopped mushrooms
¼ cup dry white wine
1 tablespoon snipped parsley
¼ teaspoon dried oregano leaves,
  crushed
  Hot cooked noodles
  Grated Parmesan cheese

Combine egg, milk, crumbs, salt, and pepper. Add veal; mix well. Shape into 6 patties; coat lightly with flour. Brown in hot oil in skillet. (Electric skillet 350°.) Drain off fat. Combine tomato sauce, *undrained* mushrooms, wine, parsley, and oregano; pour over meat. Cover; simmer 20 to 25 minutes. Serve over noodles; sprinkle with cheese. Makes 6 servings.

Saucy Sausage-Beef Burgers

COST-CUTTING RECIPE

3 tablespoons milk
1½ cups soft bread crumbs
  (1½ slices bread)
½ teaspoon poultry seasoning
½ pound bulk pork sausage
½ pound ground beef
2 tablespoons all-purpose flour
¼ teaspoon paprika
1 10½-ounce can condensed cream of
  mushroom soup
3 English muffins, split and toasted

Combine milk, crumbs, and poultry seasoning. Add sausage and beef; mix well. Shape into 6 patties. Brown slowly in skillet. (Electric skillet 350°.) Drain off fat. Stir flour and paprika into soup; gradually blend in 1 cup water. Pour around patties; cook over medium-low heat (275°) till meat is done, 15 to 20 minutes, stirring occasionally. Serve one burger on each English muffin half. Spoon mushroom sauce over top. Makes 6 servings.

Potato Schnitzel

1½ pounds veal round steak or cutlets,
  cut ½ inch thick
2 beaten eggs
2 cups instant mashed potato flakes
  or buds
½ cup grated Parmesan cheese
¼ cup cooking oil
  Lemon wedges

Cut meat into 6 serving-sized pieces; pound to ⅛-inch thickness. Cut slits in fat edges to prevent curling. Combine eggs and 2 tablespoons water; stir together dry potatoes and cheese. Dip each piece of veal in egg mixture, then in potato mixture; repeat dipping to give each a second coating. In skillet brown the meat in hot oil 3 minutes on each side. (Electric skillet 350°.) Serve with lemon. Makes 6 servings.

Mock Chicken-Fried Steak

1 beaten egg
¼ cup milk
1 cup coarsely crushed saltine
    crackers (20 crackers)
2 tablespoons finely chopped onion
1 teaspoon chili powder
¼ teaspoon salt
¼ teaspoon Worcestershire sauce
1 pound lean ground beef
2 tablespoons cooking oil
    Warmed catsup

Combine egg, milk, ½ *cup* crumbs, onion, chili powder, salt, and Worcestershire. Add beef; mix well. Shape into 6 patties, ½ inch thick; coat with remaining crumbs. In skillet cook the patties in hot oil over medium-high heat about 3 minutes on each side. (Electric skillet 325°.) Serve with catsup. Makes 6 servings.

Stuffed Beef Rolls

2 pounds ground beef
2 beaten eggs
¾ teaspoon salt
½ cup fine dry bread crumbs
2 tablespoons chopped onion
½ teaspoon ground sage
⅛ teaspoon pepper
⅓ cup water
2 tablespoons all-purpose flour
2 tablespoons cooking oil
2 10½-ounce cans condensed cream of
    mushroom soup
2 tablespoons snipped parsley
2 tablespoons chopped canned pimiento
1 3-ounce can sliced mushrooms

Mix together beef, eggs, and ½ *teaspoon* salt. Combine crumbs, onion, sage, pepper, remaining salt, and water. Divide meat into 8 portions. Pat each to 4-inch square on waxed paper; top with 2 tablespoons stuffing. Roll; seal. Coat with flour. In heavy skillet brown the meat in hot oil. (Electric skillet 350°.) Remove meat; drain off excess fat. In same skillet bring mushroom soup, parsley, pimiento, and *undrained* mushrooms to boiling. Add meat; reduce heat (220°). Cover and simmer 25 minutes, stirring occasionally. Makes 8 servings.

Meatballs in Spanish Rice

½ cup soft bread crumbs
½ cup milk
¼ cup chopped onion
1 teaspoon salt
½ teaspoon dried thyme leaves, crushed
    Dash pepper
1½ pounds ground beef
2 tablespoons cooking oil
          • • •
1½ cups uncooked packaged precooked rice
1 28-ounce can tomatoes, cut up
¼ cup water
¼ cup chopped green pepper
1 teaspoon salt

Combine first 6 ingredients; add meat and mix well. Shape into 18 balls. In large skillet brown the meatballs on all sides in hot oil. (Electric skillet 350°.) Remove meatballs and pour off excess fat. Combine remaining ingredients in skillet. Arrange meatballs on top of rice mixture. Cover and reduce heat (220°). Simmer till rice is tender and meatballs are done, about 15 minutes. Makes 6 servings.

Minute Steaks Parmesan

Mix grated Parmesan cheese with cracker crumbs to give a crispy coating to the outside of these steaks and to keep them moist and tender inside—

1 egg
1 tablespoon water
    Dash pepper
¼ cup finely crushed saltine crackers
    (6 or 7 crackers)
¼ cup grated Parmesan cheese
5 beef cube steaks (about 4
    ounces each)
2 tablespoons cooking oil
1 8-ounce can pizza sauce

Beat together egg, water, and pepper. Combine crumbs and *half* the cheese. Dip steaks in egg mixture, then in crumbs. In skillet brown the steaks in hot oil. (Electric skillet 350°.) Drain off fat. Pour in pizza sauce. Cover; reduce heat (220°). Simmer 20 minutes, adding a little water, if necessary, to keep the sauce from sticking. Sprinkle with the remaining cheese. Serves 5.

Pineapple-Plum-Glazed Pork Chops

Pictured on the cover—

6 loin pork chops, cut ½ inch thick
    (1¾ pounds)
1 20-ounce can pineapple chunks
    (juice pack)
½ cup plum jam
1 tablespoon vinegar
1 tablespoon soy sauce
¼ teaspoon ground ginger
4 green onions, sliced (¼ cup)

Trim fat from chops and melt in skillet till 1 tablespoon fat accumulates. (Electric skillet 350°.) Discard trimmings; brown the chops well on both sides in drippings. Reduce heat (220°). Season with salt and pepper. Drain pineapple chunks, reserving juice.

Combine ½ *cup* juice, the jam, vinegar, soy sauce, and ginger; pour over chops. Cover and simmer 25 minutes, adding ¼ cup more juice, if needed. Remove cover; add pineapple and onions. Spoon pan juices over them. Cover and cook till pineapple is heated through. Serves 6.

Sausage-Hominy Skillet

1 8-ounce package brown-and-
    serve sausage links, halved
2 tablespoons chopped onion
1 tablespoon butter or margarine
2 tablespoons all-purpose flour
¼ teaspoon salt
    Dash pepper
1 16-ounce can hominy, undrained
1 6-ounce can evaporated milk or
    one 2½-ounce package sour cream
    sauce mix, prepared according
    to package directions
¼ cup chopped green pepper

In skillet brown the sausage pieces. (Electric skillet 350°.) Add onion and butter; cook till onion is tender but not brown. Combine flour, salt, and pepper. Stir into sausage. Add *undrained* hominy and evaporated milk or sour cream sauce. Reduce heat (220°); cook and stir till thickened and bubbly. Add green pepper; cook till crisp-tender, about 10 minutes. Makes 4 servings.

Gingered Ham and Deviled Potatoes

1 fully cooked center cut ham slice,
    1 inch thick (about 1½ pounds)
Instant mashed potatoes (enough
    for 4 servings)
½ cup dairy sour cream
1 teaspoon prepared mustard
½ teaspoon salt
½ teaspoon sugar
2 tablespoons chopped green onion
    Paprika
⅓ cup orange marmalade
¼ teaspoon ground ginger
⅛ teaspoon ground cloves

Slash fat edge of ham slice. Panfry in electric skillet at 300° about 10 minutes. Prepare potatoes according to package directions. Stir in sour cream, mustard, salt, sugar, and green onion. Spoon into 5 foil baking shells. Sprinkle with paprika. Place in skillet. Turn ham and fry 10 minutes more. Combine marmalade, ginger, and cloves. Spoon over ham. Continue heating till ham is glazed and potatoes are heated through, 2 or 3 minutes more. Serves 5.

Ham Steak Grill

Cut a 1-pound ham steak, ½ inch thick, into 4 serving-sized pieces. In large skillet cook 4 slices bacon till crisp; set aside. (Electric skillet 350°.) Pour off all but 1 tablespoon drippings. In same skillet brown the ham on both sides in reserved drippings. Drain one 8½-ounce can pineapple slices, reserving syrup. Place 1 pineapple slice on each piece of ham. Combine 3 tablespoons brown sugar and reserved syrup; add to ham. Cover and reduce heat (220°). Simmer 15 minutes. Spoon syrup over ham and pineapple; top each with a slice of sharp process American cheese and bacon. Cover and cook till cheese melts, 1 or 2 minutes. Serves 4.

Ham steak for dinner

*A center cut ham slice weighing 1 to 1½ pounds is →
ideal for serving a small family. Panfry* Gingered Ham *and heat* Deviled Potatoes *in your electric skillet at the same time for dinner in a hurry.*

Potluck Beans

Serve with cheese wedges and fruit—

- 1 16- or 18-ounce can baked beans
- 1 16-ounce can cut green beans, drained
- 1 8½-ounce can green lima beans
- 2 teaspoons instant minced onion
- 1 12-ounce package smoked sausage links, bias-sliced

Combine baked beans, cut green beans, *undrained* lima beans, and onion in a 10-inch skillet. Stir in smoked sausage slices. Cook over medium heat, stirring occasionally, till beans are heated through, 10 to 15 minutes. (Electric skillet 350°.) Makes 4 servings.

Rice-Ham Medley

- ⅔ cup long grain rice, cooked (2 cups)
- ½ cup diced celery
- 1 4½-ounce can deviled ham
- 1 beaten egg

• • •

- ½ cup shredded natural Cheddar cheese (2 ounces)
- 2 slices bacon, crisp-cooked, drained, and crumbled

Combine rice, celery, ham, and egg in skillet. (Electric skillet 350°.) Cook and stir over medium heat till heated through, about 10 minutes. Top with cheese and bacon. Cover and cook over low heat till cheese melts, about 5 minutes more. Makes 4 servings.

Potluck Beans *is a versatile dish to which you may add or subtract at will. Substitute yellow wax beans for green in this three-bean combo, and franks or cubed, canned luncheon meat for the smoked sausage.*

Swissed Vegetables on Toast

    2 16-ounce cans mixed vegetables
    ¼ cup all-purpose flour
    1 3-ounce package cream cheese,
       cut in cubes
    ¼ cup milk
    ¼ teaspoon onion powder
         • • •
    2 cups fully cooked ham, cut in
       ½-inch cubes
    ½ cup shredded process Swiss cheese
       (2 ounces)
    Toast points

In 10-inch skillet stir *undrained* mixed vegetables into flour. (Electric skillet 350°.) Add cream cheese, milk, and onion powder; cook and stir over medium heat till mixture is thickened and bubbly. Stir in cubed ham and shredded Swiss cheese; cook till cheese melts. Serve over toast points. Makes 6 servings.

Veal Paprika

    1½ pounds boneless veal shoulder,
       cut in 1-inch cubes
    2 tablespoons butter or margarine
    1½ cups chopped onion
    1¾ cups water
    1 16-ounce can tomatoes, cut up
    2 tablespoons paprika
    1½ teaspoons salt
    1 teaspoon sugar
    ½ teaspoon dried marjoram leaves,
       crushed
         • • •
    8 ounces medium noodles (6 cups)
    1½ tablespoons all-purpose flour
    1 cup dairy sour cream

In a 12-inch skillet brown the veal in butter. (Electric skillet 350°.) Add chopped onion; cook and stir till onion is tender but not brown. Add water, tomatoes, paprika, salt, sugar, and marjoram. Cover; simmer, stirring occasionally, 30 to 35 minutes. Cook noodles according to package directions; drain and keep warm. Stir flour into sour cream. Stir a small amount of the veal mixture into sour cream. Slowly add sour cream to veal mixture in skillet; stir to combine. Serve over the hot cooked noodles. Makes 4 servings.

Polish Potato Salad

To brown evenly, start the bacon in a cold skillet—

    4 slices bacon
    ¾ cup chopped onion
    3 tablespoons all-purpose flour
    ⅓ cup sugar
    1½ teaspoons salt
    ¾ teaspoon celery seed
       Dash pepper
    ¾ cup water
    ¾ cup vinegar
    8 medium potatoes, cooked, peeled,
       and cubed (5 cups)
    18 ounces Polish sausage, bias-sliced
    3 tablespoons snipped parsley

In skillet cook bacon till crisp. (Electric skillet 350°.) Drain and crumble, reserving 2 tablespoons drippings. Reduce heat. Cook onion in reserved drippings till tender but not brown. Stir in flour, sugar, salt, celery seed, and pepper. Add water and vinegar; cook and stir till thickened and bubbly. Stir in potatoes and sliced Polish sausage. Cover the skillet; reduce heat (220°) and simmer, stirring once or twice, till potatoes are heated through, 5 to 10 minutes. Top with crumbled bacon. Sprinkle with parsley. Makes 6 servings.

Rickshaw Rice

A canned meat and vegetable medley—

    1 12-ounce can luncheon meat, cubed
    2 tablespoons butter or margarine
    1 20½-ounce can pineapple chunks
    ⅔ cup long grain rice, cooked (2 cups)
    1 10-ounce package frozen peas
    1 teaspoon dried dillweed, crushed
    1 cup cherry tomatoes, halved
    ½ cup dairy sour cream

In skillet brown the meat in butter. (Electric skillet 350°.) Drain pineapple, reserving ¾ cup syrup. Add pineapple, reserved syrup, rice, peas, and dillweed to skillet. Cover the skillet; reduce heat (220°) and simmer till peas are tender, 4 to 5 minutes. Stir in tomatoes. Top with sour cream. Cover and simmer till tomatoes are hot, 2 minutes more. Makes 4 to 6 servings.

Chicken-Fried Rice

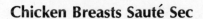

2 well-beaten eggs
2 tablespoons butter
1 cup uncooked long grain rice
3 tablespoons cooking oil
1 10½-ounce can condensed
    chicken broth
1¼ cups water
1 cup finely diced, cooked chicken
3 tablespoons soy sauce
½ cup sliced fresh or canned mushrooms
2 tablespoons thinly sliced green
    onions with tops

In skillet over medium heat, cook eggs in butter, without stirring, till set. (Electric skillet 300°.) Remove from skillet; cut into thin strips. Keep warm. In same skillet over medium heat, brown the rice in oil. Add broth, water, chicken, and soy sauce. Cover and reduce heat (220°). Simmer till rice is tender and liquids are absorbed, about 20 to 30 minutes. Stir in mushrooms and green onions. Cook over low heat, stirring occasionally, till mushrooms are cooked. Top with egg strips before serving. Serves 6.

Chicken Livers and Apple Slices

3 tablespoons all-purpose flour
¾ teaspoon salt
¾ teaspoon paprika
¾ teaspoon dried sage leaves,
    crushed
1 pound chicken livers (about 12)
1 medium onion, sliced (½ cup)
3 tablespoons butter or margarine
1 apple, cored and sliced ½-inch thick
2 tablespoons sugar (optional)
    Toast points

Combine flour, salt, paprika, and sage in paper or plastic bag. Cut large livers in half; add ⅓ of the livers at a time; shake to coat well. Set aside. In heavy skillet cook onion in *2 tablespoons* of the butter till tender but not brown. (Electric skillet 300°.) Push onion to one side and brown the livers lightly, 5 or 6 minutes. Push to one side. Add remaining 1 tablespoon butter and apple slices; cook till tender, about 5 minutes. Sprinkle apples with sugar to glaze. Serve with toast. Makes 4 servings.

Chicken Breasts Sauté Sec

3 chicken breasts (2 pounds)
1 tablespoon lemon juice
¼ cup all-purpose flour
1 teaspoon salt
1 teaspoon paprika
    Dash freshly ground pepper
3 tablespoons butter or margarine
1 clove garlic, halved
½ cup dry white wine
    Golden Sauce

Skin and split chicken breasts; rub with lemon juice. Combine flour, salt, paprika, and pepper in paper or plastic bag; add 2 or 3 pieces of chicken at a time and shake to coat well. Heat butter and garlic in heavy skillet. (Electric skillet 300°.) Discard garlic. Cook chicken till golden on both sides; add wine. Cover and reduce heat (220°). Simmer till tender, about 20 minutes. Uncover; cook till pan liquid is reduced to ¼ cup, about 10 minutes longer. Remove chicken to platter and keep hot.

Golden Sauce: In saucepan combine pan liquid, 4 beaten egg yolks, 1 cup whipping cream, 1 tablespoon *each* snipped parsley and chives, and ⅛ teaspoon ground nutmeg. Season with salt and white pepper. Cook and stir over low heat till slightly thickened. Add ½ teaspoon lemon juice; pour over chicken. Serves 4.

Hot Chicken Stroganoff Salad

1 6-ounce package long grain and wild
    rice mix
2 cups cubed, cooked chicken
1 cup sliced celery
¾ cup dairy sour cream
¼ cup mayonnaise
½ cup milk
½ teaspoon salt
¼ cup coarsely chopped cashew nuts
    Parsley sprigs

In skillet cook rice mix according to package directions; add chicken and celery. Blend sour cream, mayonnaise, milk, and salt. Stir into chicken-rice mixture. Cook and stir over low heat till mixture heats through. (Electric skillet 220°.) Add more milk, if desired; garnish with cashews and parsley. Makes 6 servings.

Cooked chicken-in-a-hurry

For any recipe calling for 2 cups cubed or diced, cooked chicken, or 12 thin slices cooked chicken, buy 2 whole chicken breasts (about 10 ounces each). In 10-inch skillet combine chicken breasts and 2½ cups salted water or chicken broth. Bring to boiling. (Electric skillet 350°.) Reduce heat, cover, and simmer till tender, about 20 minutes. Do not overcook.

In addition to cooking quickly, chicken breasts are almost all meat, so are more economical than bonier pieces for casseroles, salads, or sandwiches. They are also tender.

Chicken Skillet Pie

Old favorite tamale pie updated for use in an electric skillet. It has refrigerator biscuits on top instead of cooked cornmeal around the sides—

    1 pound ground beef
    ¾ cup chopped onion
    1 15-ounce can tomato sauce
    2 cups diced, cooked chicken or turkey
    ½ cup pitted ripe olives, halved
    ½ cup shredded sharp process
        American cheese
    ½ teaspoon ground oregano
    1 chicken bouillon cube
    1 package refrigerated buttermilk
        biscuits (5 biscuits)
    2 tablespoons butter, melted
    ¼ cup cornmeal

In heavy skillet cook the beef and onion till meat is browned and onion is tender. (Electric skillet 350°.) Add tomato sauce, chicken, olives, cheese, and oregano. Dissolve bouillon in 1 cup boiling water; add to meat mixture. Cover and reduce heat (220°). Simmer 15 minutes, closing vent on electric skillet.

Dip both sides of refrigerator biscuits in butter; coat with cornmeal. Place on top of meat mixture. Cover and cook till biscuits are done, about 15 minutes. Makes 5 servings.

Jambalaya

The Creoles added French jambon (ham) to a Spanish paella of rice and chicken to make this dish—

    3 slices bacon
    ½ cup uncooked long grain rice
    1 medium onion, chopped (½ cup)
    1 13¾-ounce can chicken broth
        (1¾ cups)
    1 8-ounce can tomato sauce
    2 cups cubed, cooked chicken
    1 cup cubed, fully cooked ham
    ½ teaspoon salt
    Dash freshly ground pepper

In skillet cook bacon. (Electric skillet 350°.) Drain on paper toweling; crumble and set aside. Add rice and onion to drippings and cook till golden, stirring frequently. Reduce heat (220°). Add chicken broth, tomato sauce, chicken, ham, salt, and pepper. Cover and simmer till rice is tender, about 25 minutes, adding more water if necessary. Stir in bacon. Serves 6.

French-Toasted Chicken Sandwiches

    2 cups chopped, cooked chicken
        or turkey
    ½ cup finely chopped celery
    ⅓ cup mayonnaise or salad dressing
    3 tablespoons sweet pickle relish
    2 tablespoons finely chopped onion
    ½ teaspoon salt
        Dash pepper
    12 slices white bread
    2 beaten eggs
    ½ cup milk
    3 cups potato chips, crushed
        (1½ cups)
    ¼ cup butter or margarine
        Seedless green grapes (optional)

Combine chicken, celery, mayonnaise, pickle relish, onion, salt, and pepper. Spread 6 slices of bread with about ⅓ cup of the mixture; cover with remaining bread. Combine eggs and milk in pie plate. Dip sandwiches on both sides, then coat with potato chips. In heavy skillet cook in hot butter till brown on both sides, about 5 minutes per side. (Electric skillet 350°.) Serve with seedless green grapes, if desired. Serves 6.

Coatings for fish

Dip fish in seasoned flour, then in egg mixed with water to make one of the following coatings stick:
- Try ¼ cup grated Parmesan cheese combined with 1 cup saltine cracker crumbs on 6 pan-dressed fish.
- Combine 1 cup instant mashed potato flakes with 1 envelope onion salad dressing mix for 4 pan-dressed fish.
- Use ¾ cup cornmeal, ½ teaspoon salt, and dash pepper for 4 pan-dressed fish. Use hot bacon drippings for extra flavor when frying.
- Mix together ⅓ cup all-purpose flour, ½ teaspoon paprika, ¼ teaspoon salt, and dash pepper; roll 4 pan-dressed fish in it and fry in butter.

Oyster Cakes Hollandaise

Make and chill cakes early; brown before serving—

    2 tablespoons finely chopped onion
    ¼ cup butter or margarine
    2 beaten eggs
    3 cups soft bread crumbs
    1 pint oysters, drained and chopped
    ½ cup finely chopped celery
    ¼ cup milk
    2 tablespoons snipped parsley
    1 tablespoon lemon juice
    ½ teaspoon salt
    ½ teaspoon paprika
    ¾ cup fine dry bread crumbs
    1 1¾-ounce envelope hollandaise
       sauce mix

In skillet cook onion in *2 tablespoons* butter till tender but not brown. (Electric skillet 350°.) Combine with eggs, soft bread crumbs, oysters, celery, milk, parsley, lemon juice, salt, and paprika. Shape into 8 patties ½ inch thick. Coat with fine dry crumbs. Chill. In skillet melt remaining butter. Brown the cakes. Reduce heat (220°) and cook 6 to 8 minutes. Prepare hollandaise sauce according to package directions; serve over cakes. Makes 4 servings.

Crab and Avocado

    ¼ cup butter or margarine
    ¼ cup all-purpose flour
    ½ teaspoon salt
    ½ teaspoon prepared mustard
    2 cups milk
    2 6-ounce packages frozen crab meat,
       thawed, or 2 7½-ounce cans crab
       meat, drained and cartilage removed
    1 3-ounce can sliced mushrooms, drained
    3 tablespoons dry white wine
       Few drops bottled hot pepper sauce
    1 large ripe avocado, peeled and cut
       in 6 wedges
    1 tablespoon lemon or lime juice
       Garlic salt
    ½ cup shredded process American cheese
       (2 ounces)

Melt butter in blazer pan of chafing dish. Blend in flour, salt, and mustard; add milk all at once. Cook and stir till thickened and bubbly. Stir in crab, mushrooms, wine, and hot pepper sauce; heat through. Brush avocado with lemon juice; sprinkle with garlic salt. Add remaining lemon juice to crab mixture.

Place avocado on crab. Sprinkle with cheese. Cover and continue cooking till the cheese melts, 4 or 5 minutes. Makes 6 servings.

Halibut in Wine

    1 pound fresh or frozen halibut steaks
    ⅓ cup dry white wine
    ½ onion, sliced
    ½ cup sliced celery
    ¼ cup butter or margarine
    1 tablespoon snipped parsley
    1 teaspoon Worcestershire sauce
    ¼ teaspoon dried basil leaves, crushed
    1 cup cherry tomatoes, halved

Thaw frozen fish. Sprinkle with salt and pepper. Place in shallow dish; add wine. Let stand 30 minutes; turn once. In medium skillet cook onion and celery in butter till tender. (Electric skillet 300°.) Stir in parsley, Worcestershire, and basil. Add fish and wine. Cover; reduce heat (220°); cook 10 minutes. Add tomatoes. Cover and cook till fish flakes easily when tested with a fork, 3 or 4 minutes more. Serves 4.

Here's a delicious dish, Crab and Avocado *in a wine sauce. It goes well with crisp green salad—use several kinds of greens—and hot, buttered French bread. Honeydew melon rounds out this special occasion meal.*

Scallops Amandine

¾ **pound fresh or frozen scallops**
⅓ **cup all-purpose flour**
¼ **teaspoon salt**
¼ **cup butter or margarine**
3 **tablespoons slivered almonds**
1 **tablespoon lemon juice**
1 **tablespoon snipped parsley**

Thaw frozen scallops; cut large scallops in thick slices. Coat with a mixture of flour and salt. In skillet cook in *2 tablespoons* of the butter till golden, about 5 minutes. (Electric skillet 350°.) Remove to warm serving platter. Melt remaining butter; add almonds and toast till golden. Stir in lemon juice and parsley; pour over scallops. Makes 4 servings.

Pan-Fried Fish

2 **pounds fresh or frozen fish**
   fillets, steaks, or
   pan-dressed fish
1 **beaten egg**
2 **tablespoons water**
¾ **cup fine saltine cracker crumbs**
   Shortening

Thaw frozen fish. Cut fillets or steaks into 6 portions. Dip into mixture of egg and water, then roll in crumbs. Heat shortening in skillet. (Electric skillet 300°.) Brown on one side, 4 or 5 minutes. Turn; brown till fish flakes easily with a fork, 4 or 5 minutes. Drain on paper toweling. Makes 6 servings of fillets or steaks; 4 of pan-dressed fish.

Bahamian Chowder

1 16-ounce can tomatoes,
cut up (2 cups)
1 cup water
½ cup diced, peeled potato
¼ cup diced green pepper
¼ cup diced onion
¼ cup diced celery
¼ teaspoon garlic salt
¼ teaspoon chili powder

• • •

1 cup diced, fully cooked ham
1 7½-ounce can minced clams
1 tablespoon butter or margarine

In skillet combine first 8 ingredients. (Electric skillet 220°.) Cover and simmer till vegetables are tender, about 30 minutes. Add ham, *undrained* clams, and butter; simmer till mixture is heated through. Makes 4 servings.

The difference between Bahamian Chowder and Manhattan-style chowder is chili powder and ham. Both use tomatoes. New Englanders omit all three.

Salmon Skillet Goldenrod

1 cup water
1 tablespoon butter or margarine
1 cup uncooked packaged precooked rice
1 10½-ounce can condensed cream of
celery soup
¾ cup milk
2 3-ounce packages cream cheese, cubed
2 hard-cooked eggs
1 9-ounce package frozen cut asparagus,
cooked and drained
1 16-ounce can salmon, drained, flaked,
and bones removed

Bring water and butter to a boil in a small saucepan. Add rice; turn off heat. Cover and let stand 5 minutes. In a 12-inch skillet combine soup, milk, cream cheese, and rice. (Electric skillet 220°.) Cook and stir over low heat till cheese melts.

Remove yolk from one hard-cooked egg; set aside for garnish. Coarsely chop egg white and remaining egg. Fold chopped egg and asparagus into rice mixture. Simmer till mixture is heated through, about 15 minutes. Stir occasionally. Stir in salmon; heat through. Garnish with sieved egg yolk. Makes 4 to 6 servings.

Tuna Patties with Cranberry Sauce

2 eggs
¼ cup milk
1½ cups soft bread crumbs
1 tablespoon chopped
green onion
1 9½-ounce can tuna, drained and
flaked
1 tablespoon water
½ cup fine dry bread crumbs
2 tablespoons cooking oil
1 8-ounce can whole cranberry sauce

Combine *one* of the eggs, milk, soft bread crumbs, green onion, ¼ teaspoon salt, and dash pepper. Mix well. Stir in tuna. Form into 6 patties, ¾ inch thick. Beat together second egg and water. Dip patties in egg, then in dry bread crumbs. In skillet brown the patties over medium heat in hot oil, about 5 minutes. (Electric skillet 350°.) At serving time, spoon cranberry sauce over each patty. Makes 6 servings.

Curried Eggs

2 tablespoons butter
2 to 3 teaspoons curry powder
½ teaspoon salt
1 cup coarsely chopped apple
½ cup sliced green onion with tops
1 clove garlic, minced
1 10½-ounce can condensed cream of
   celery soup
⅔ cup milk
1 3-ounce can sliced mushrooms, drained
4 hard-cooked eggs, quartered
   Hot cooked rice
   Raisins
   Shredded coconut
   Chopped peanuts

In medium skillet melt butter; stir in curry powder and salt. (Electric skillet 300°.) Add apple, onion, and garlic. Cook till onion is tender, about 5 minutes. Add soup and milk; bring to a boil, stirring till smooth. Reduce heat (220°); add mushrooms. Gently fold in eggs. Cover and continue cooking till heated through. Serve over cooked rice. Pass condiments—raisins, shredded coconut, and chopped peanuts. Makes 4 servings.

Spanish Potato Omelet

2 large potatoes, peeled and
   finely chopped (3 cups)
½ cup finely chopped onion
5 tablespoons olive oil
6 beaten eggs
⅓ cup milk

In 10-inch skillet cook potatoes and onion in *3 tablespoons* of the oil till tender, turning occasionally. (Electric skillet 300°.) Season with ½ teaspoon salt. Remove from heat.

Combine eggs, milk, ½ teaspoon salt, and dash pepper. Stir in potato mixture. Heat remaining 2 tablespoons oil in same skillet. Pour in egg mixture. Cover; reduce heat (220°). Cook till omelet is nearly set, about 10 minutes. Invert omelet by placing plate over skillet and turning over. Slide the omelet back into the skillet, moist side down. Cook till underside is set, 1 or 2 minutes. Loosen and slide onto serving plate. Makes 4 servings.

Tuna Supper Dish

1 cup soft bread crumbs
¼ cup butter or margarine
1 9-ounce package frozen
   Italian green beans
2 tablespoons all-purpose flour
1⅓ cups chicken broth
⅛ teaspoon ground nutmeg
   Dash pepper
2 6½- or 7-ounce cans chunk-style
   tuna, drained
1 cup shredded process American
   cheese (4 ounces)

In heavy skillet toast the bread crumbs in *2 tablespoons* of the butter till golden brown. (Electric skillet 350°.) Set aside. Cook beans according to package directions; drain. In skillet blend flour into remaining butter. Add chicken broth, nutmeg, and pepper. Cook and stir till thick and smooth. Add tuna, cheese, and beans; reduce heat (220°). Simmer till cheese melts. Sprinkle with crumbs. Serves 4 to 6.

Tuna Omelet

3 tablespoons cooking oil
½ cup frozen peas
½ cup bean sprouts, drained
1 6½- or 7-ounce can tuna, drained
6 eggs
¼ cup water

In heavy 10-inch skillet heat the oil. (Electric skillet 350°.) Add peas, sprouts, and tuna; cook, stirring occasionally, till peas are tender, about 5 minutes. Beat eggs with water, ½ teaspoon salt, and dash pepper; pour into skillet. Reduce heat (220°); cook till eggs are set. When almost cooked but still shiny, loosen edges; fold one half over. Serves 4 to 6.

Beefy Scrambled Eggs

In heavy skillet cook one 4-ounce package sliced dried beef in 2 tablespoons butter or margarine till edges curl. (Electric skillet 350°.) Add 8 beaten eggs and one 3-ounce can sliced mushrooms, drained. Cook and stir till cooked to desired doneness. Makes 4 servings.

Danish Hamburgers

1 pound ground beef
½ cup mashed potatoes
¾ teaspoon salt
    Dash freshly ground pepper
½ cup crumbled blue cheese (2 ounces)
1 tablespoon butter or margarine
3 hamburger buns, split and toasted
6 cherry tomatoes
6 whole mushrooms
6 Boston or Bibb lettuce leaves

Combine ground beef, mashed potatoes, salt, and pepper; mix thoroughly. Shape into 12 thin patties, about 4 inches in diameter; place a spoonful of blue cheese on 6 patties; top with remaining patties, pinching edges together so cheese will not run out. Brown in hot butter in heavy skillet over medium-high heat about 4 or 5 minutes per side. (Electric skillet 350°.) Serve open-face on toasted bun halves; garnish with tomato, mushroom, and lettuce leaf on cocktail pick. Makes 6 servings.

French Hamburgers

¼ cup milk
1 egg
¼ cup sharp process cheese
    spread, softened
¼ cup mayonnaise or salad dressing
3 tablespoons thinly sliced green onion
½ teaspoon mixed salad herbs, crushed
¼ teaspoon seasoned salt
1½ cups shredded lettuce
8 slices boiled ham (8 ounces)
4 sesame seed hamburger buns or 8
    slices rye bread
¼ cup butter or margarine
    Sliced tomatoes

Gradually beat milk and egg into cheese spread. Set aside. Combine mayonnaise, onion, salad herbs, and seasoned salt; mix with lettuce. Place two 1-ounce ham slices on bun half or bread slice. Top with lettuce mixture and close bun or add second slice bread. Dip in cheese-milk mixture and brown on both sides in melted butter in skillet, about 5 minutes. (Electric skillet 350°.) Serve immediately with sliced tomatoes. Makes 4 servings.

Budget Barbecues

½ cup chopped onion
2 tablespoons butter
1 cup catsup
⅓ cup brown sugar
¼ cup water
2 tablespoons vinegar
1 tablespoon Worcestershire sauce
1 teaspoon dry mustard
1 teaspoon paprika
½ teaspoon chili powder
    • • •
1 8-ounce can sauerkraut, drained and
    snipped
2 cups leftover, cooked beef or ham,
    cut in thin strips
    Hamburger buns, split and toasted

In skillet cook onion in butter till tender but not brown. (Electric skillet 300°.) Blend in catsup, brown sugar, water, vinegar, Worcestershire sauce, mustard, paprika, and chili powder; bring to boiling. Add sauerkraut. Cover; reduce heat (220°) and simmer about 10 minutes. Add meat. Simmer, uncovered, till meat heats through and barbecue sauce thickens. Serve on toasted buns. Makes 8 to 12 sandwiches.

Cheese-Bacon-Tomato Sandwiches

    Butter or margarine, softened
8 slices sandwich bread
4 slices mozzarella cheese
⅓ cup dairy sour cream
2 tablespoons chopped onion
2 tomatoes, sliced
    Dried oregano leaves, crushed
    Seasoned salt
8 slices bacon, crisp cooked and
    drained

Butter bread on both sides. For each sandwich, top 1 slice of bread with a cheese slice, a dollop of sour cream, chopped onion, and tomato slices. Sprinkle with oregano and seasoned salt. Add 2 slices bacon; top with another bread slice. Place sandwich, cheese side down, in skillet. Cover and cook till the bread is golden brown and the cheese is melted. (Electric skillet 350°.) Turn sandwich; cover and brown on other side. Makes 4 sandwiches.

Grilled German Bratburgers

4 bratwurst links (12 ounces)
1½ cups coarsely chopped onion
1 12-ounce can beer (1½ cups)
½ cup shredded sharp natural Cheddar
   cheese (2 ounces)
4 frankfurter buns, buttered
4 slices bacon, crisp-cooked,
   drained, and crumbled

In 10-inch skillet brown the bratwurst over medium heat. (Electric skillet 300°.) Add onion and beer; simmer, uncovered, for 20 to 30 minutes. Remove links; slit each lengthwise. Discard beer. Fill with cheese; place in buns. Place each in a foil 'boat,' leaving cheese side open. Return to skillet; cover and heat (250°) till cheese melts, about 2 minutes. Top with bacon. Serves 4.

Beer-Kraut Heroes

1 beaten egg
¼ cup fine dry bread crumbs
1 cup beer
¾ teaspoon salt
1 pound ground beef
2 tablespoons cooking oil
1 cup thinly sliced onion
2 tablespoons snipped parsley
⅛ teaspoon dried thyme leaves, crushed
1 small bay leaf
1 beef bouillon cube
1 16-ounce can sauerkraut, drained
1 tablespoon cornstarch
2 tablespoons cold water
4 hero rolls, split, toasted, and
   buttered

Combine egg, crumbs, ¼ *cup* of the beer, salt, and dash pepper; add ground beef and mix well. Shape into 20 meatballs. In heavy skillet brown the meatballs in hot oil. (Electric skillet 350°.) Add onion, parsley, thyme, bay leaf, bouillon cube, and the remaining beer. Reduce heat (220°); simmer, covered, for 20 minutes. Meanwhile, heat sauerkraut. Remove meatballs from skillet; cover and keep warm. Blend cornstarch and water; add to pan juices. Cook and stir till thickened. Place sauerkraut on rolls; top with meatballs. Pour thickened broth over all. Makes 4 servings.

Baconwiches with Hot Apple Syrup

8 slices bacon
2 slightly beaten eggs
¾ cup milk
¼ teaspoon salt
8 slices bread
   Hot Apple Syrup

In skillet cook bacon till crisp. (Electric skillet 350°.) Drain bacon; reserve drippings. Combine eggs, milk, and salt. Dip bread in mixture; fry in drippings till brown. Crumble bacon over 4 toast slices; top with remaining toast. Pass Hot Apple Syrup. Serves 4.

Hot Apple Syrup: In small skillet melt ½ cup apple jelly and 2 tablespoons butter with ⅛ teaspoon ground cinnamon; stir till smooth.

Give Baconwiches a coating of eggs and milk and a French toasting to make them more nutritious than most luncheon sandwiches. Pass Hot Apple Syrup.

Huevos Rancheros (Ranch-Style Eggs)

Heat remaining half package of tortillas for bread; butter and roll or fold in quarters to eat—

¼ cup cooking oil
6 frozen tortillas, thawed
    (½ of a 9-ounce package)
½ cup chopped onion
1 small clove garlic, minced
2 tablespoons cooking oil
3 large tomatoes, peeled, cored,
    and finely chopped
¼ cup green chilies, drained, rinsed,
    seeded, and chopped (2 chilies)
¼ teaspoon salt
6 eggs
1 cup shredded Monterey Jack cheese

Heat ¼ cup oil in a medium skillet. (Electric skillet 250°.) Dip tortillas in oil for a few seconds till softened but not brown. Keep warm. In same skillet cook onion and garlic in 2 tablespoons oil till tender but not brown. Add tomatoes, chilies, and ¼ teaspoon salt. Simmer 10 minutes. Slide eggs into tomato mixture, taking care not to break yolks. Season with salt and pepper. Cover skillet and cook eggs till of desired doneness. Place an egg with some of the tomato mixture on each tortilla. Top with shredded cheese. Makes 6 servings.

Barbecued Steaks and Beans

4 beef minute steaks (1 pound)
¼ cup chopped onion
1 tablespoon cooking oil
1 16-ounce can home-style pork
    and beans
½ cup bottled barbecue sauce
½ teaspoon garlic salt
½ teaspoon dried oregano leaves,
    crushed
¼ cup shredded sharp process American
    cheese (1 ounce)

In 10-inch skillet brown the steaks with onion in oil 1 minute per side. (Electric skillet 350°.) Add beans, barbecue sauce, garlic salt, and oregano. Reduce heat (220°). Cover; simmer 10 minutes. Sprinkle with cheese. Cover; heat just till cheese melts. Makes 4 servings.

Mexican Skillet Spaghetti

1 pound ground beef
1 15-ounce can tomato sauce
4¾ cups water (2½ tomato-sauce cans)
2 1¼-ounce packages taco mix
2 tablespoons instant minced onion
½ teaspoon salt
    • • •
8 ounces uncooked spaghetti
½ cup shredded natural Cheddar cheese

In 12-inch skillet brown the ground beef. (Electric skillet 350°.) Add tomato sauce, water, taco mix, instant minced onion, and salt. Bring mixture to boiling; add spaghetti. Reduce heat (220°). Simmer, covered, until the spaghetti is tender, stirring frequently, about 25 to 30 minutes. Sprinkle with shredded cheese. Serves 6.

Chicken Tamale Pie

1 10¾-ounce can Cheddar cheese soup
1 8-ounce can tomato sauce
2 5-ounce cans boned chicken
¾ cup uncooked packaged precooked rice
2 15-ounce cans tamales

In medium skillet combine cheese soup, tomato sauce, chicken, and rice. (Electric skillet 220°.) Cover; simmer over low heat 5 minutes. Place tamales atop mixture in skillet. Cover; cook till tamales are heated through, about 10 minutes. Makes 4 to 6 servings.

Skillet Breakfast Pie

4 slices bacon
1 12-ounce package frozen
    loose-pack hashed brown potatoes,
    or 2 cups diced fresh potatoes
4 eggs

In an 8-inch skillet cook bacon till crisp. (Electric skillet 350°.) Remove bacon and cook potatoes in drippings till golden brown. Season with salt and pepper. Place bacon across potatoes to divide top into 4 portions. Break an egg into each portion. Reduce heat (220°). Cover and cook just till eggs are set, about 10 minutes. Makes 2 large servings.

Convenience foods are a boon for campers. Being lightweight, with half the preparation done, they make possible quick suppers like this Mexican Skillet Spaghetti. *It's seasoned with two packages of taco mix.*

Spicy Apricot-Glazed Pork Chops
(190 calories per serving)

        6 lean pork loin chops, cut ½ inch
            thick (about 2 pounds)
    ½ cup low-calorie apricot preserves
      1 tablespoon vinegar
      ¼ teaspoon ground cinnamon
      ⅛ teaspoon ground nutmeg
        Dash ground cloves

Trim excess fat from chops. In skillet panbroil chops over medium heat. (Electric skillet 300°.) Turn chops occasionally till done, about 15 to 20 minutes. Season chops with salt and pepper. Pour off any drippings. Combine preserves, 2 tablespoons water, vinegar, ¼ teaspoon salt, and spices. Spoon over chops. Heat till bubbly. Makes 6 servings.

Beef-Kraut Skillet
(280 calories per serving)

      1 pound lean ground beef
    1¼ teaspoons salt
      1 teaspoon brown sugar
    ½ teaspoon dried sage leaves, crushed
      1 8½-ounce can pineapple tidbits
            (juice pack)
      1 8-ounce can sauerkraut, undrained
      1 unpeeled medium apple, sliced
      1 teaspoon cornstarch

In skillet brown the ground beef. (Electric skillet 350°.) Drain off excess fat. Stir in salt, brown sugar, sage, and ⅛ teaspoon pepper. Add pineapple with juice, sauerkraut, and ½ cup water. Cover; reduce heat (220°). Simmer 15 to 20 minutes, stirring occasionally. Add apple. Cook, covered, 10 minutes more. Combine ¼ cup cold water and cornstarch; stir into skillet mixture. Cook and stir gently till thickened and bubbly. Makes 4 servings.

Low-calorie eating at its best

← *Prepare Pineapple-Poached Fish for those who are counting calories. Accompany the skillet dish with cucumber sticks. It's so tasty that the whole family will enjoy this vegetable-fish combination.*

Pineapple-Poached Fish
(160 calories per serving)

      1 cup unsweetened pineapple juice
      1 tablespoon vinegar
      1 tablespoon soy sauce
      1 cup celery cut in ¼-inch pieces
      2 medium carrots, thinly sliced
                • • •
      1 pound frozen flounder or sole fillets,
            thawed
      1 tablespoon cornstarch
      1 cup cherry tomatoes, halved

In medium skillet combine pineapple juice, vinegar, soy sauce, ¼ teaspoon salt, and dash pepper. Add celery and carrots; bring to boiling. (Electric skillet 350°.) Reduce heat (220°). Cover and simmer till crisp-tender, 8 to 10 minutes. Clear center of skillet by pushing vegetables to outer edge.

Season fish with salt; place in single layer in pineapple juice in center of skillet; bring to boiling. Cover; simmer till fish flakes easily when tested with a fork, 2 to 3 minutes. Remove fish from skillet. Combine ¼ cup cold water and cornstarch; add to pineapple juice. Cook and stir till thickened and bubbly. Add tomatoes; heat. Pass sauce with fish. Serves 4.

Chinese-Style Liver
(310 calories per serving)

      1 pound beef or calves liver
      2 teaspoons cornstarch
      ¼ teaspoon ground ginger
      2 tablespoons dry sherry
      ⅓ cup sliced green onions with tops
      1 tablespoon cooking oil
      1 5- or 6-ounce can bamboo shoots,
            drained
      1 3-ounce can sliced mushrooms, drained
      1 tablespoon soy sauce
      2 cups hot cooked rice

Cut liver into narrow strips. Combine cornstarch, ginger, sherry, and green onions; toss with liver. In medium skillet brown the liver quickly in hot oil. (Electric skillet 350°.) Add bamboo shoots and mushrooms; cook, stirring constantly, till heated through. Stir in soy sauce. Serve over rice. Makes 4 servings.

Stuffed Tomatoes
(160 calories per serving)

8 firm large tomatoes (3 pounds)
1 tablespoon cooking oil
½ cup finely chopped onion
2 cloves garlic, minced
1 pound lean ground beef
2 tablespoons snipped parsley
½ teaspoon dried thyme leaves, crushed
½ teaspoon dried sage leaves, crushed

Wash tomatoes; cut slice from bottom and scoop out pulp. Chop pulp and slices; reserve. Sprinkle salt inside of tomato shells; turn upside down to drain.

Heat oil in heavy skillet. (Electric skillet 350°.) Add onion and garlic; cook till tender but not brown. Add beef and brown. Drain off fat. Add parsley, ¾ teaspoon salt, thyme, sage, dash pepper, and reserved chopped tomato to meat. Fill tomatoes with meat; place in skillet. Add ⅓ cup water. Reduce heat (220°). Cover and simmer 15 minutes. Makes 8 servings.

Beef-Eggplant Skillet
(335 calories per serving)

1½ pounds lean ground beef
½ cup chopped onion
1 16-ounce can tomatoes, cut up
1 teaspoon garlic salt
½ teaspoon dried thyme leaves, crushed
¼ teaspoon ground cinnamon (optional)
4½ cups cubed, peeled eggplant
    (about 1 pound)
1 tablespoon all-purpose flour
1 cup process Swiss cheese, shredded
    (4 ounces)

In a skillet cook the beef and the onion till the meat is browned. (Electric skillet 350°.) Drain off fat. Stir in tomatoes, garlic salt, ½ teaspoon salt, thyme, and cinnamon. Add eggplant. Cover the skillet; reduce heat (220°). Simmer till eggplant is tender, about 10 minutes, stirring occasionally.

Combine flour and 2 tablespoons cold water; stir into skillet mixture. Cook and stir till thickened and bubbly. Sprinkle cheese atop mixture. Cover; continue heating till cheese melts, 1 or 2 minutes more. Makes 6 servings.

Dieter's Stroganoff
(305 calories per serving)

1 cup cream-style cottage cheese
1 tablespoon lemon juice
1 pound lean ground beef
¼ cup chopped onion
2 tablespoons all-purpose flour
½ teaspoon dried basil leaves, crushed
⅛ teaspoon garlic powder
1 beef bouillon cube
1 8-ounce can tomato sauce
1 3-ounce can sliced mushrooms
3 cups hot cooked noodles

Blend cottage cheese and lemon juice on low speed in blender. Gradually blend in ⅓ cup water; set aside. In skillet cook meat and onion till meat is lightly browned. (Electric skillet 350°.) Drain off fat. Combine flour, basil, garlic powder, and ⅛ teaspoon pepper; stir into meat. Dissolve bouillon in ½ cup boiling water. Stir into meat with tomato sauce and *undrained* mushrooms. Reduce heat (220°). Simmer, uncovered, 10 minutes; stir occasionally. Stir in cheese mixture. Heat (do not boil). Serve over noodles. Makes 6 servings.

Veal Cutlets
(215 calories per serving)

4 boneless veal cutlets (1 pound)
1 small clove garlic, minced
1 teaspoon cooking oil
1 chicken bouillon cube
½ teaspoon dried oregano leaves,
    crushed
1 teaspoon cornstarch
1 tablespoon snipped parsley
2 tablespoons shredded mozzarella
    cheese

Pound veal to ¼- to ⅛-inch thickness. Sprinkle lightly with salt. In 8-inch skillet brown the veal and garlic quickly in oil. Dissolve bouillon cube in ½ cup boiling water. Add oregano; pour over meat. Reduce heat. Simmer, covered, 10 to 12 minutes. Remove meat; keep warm. Combine cornstarch and 1 tablespoon cold water; add to pan juices. Cook and stir till thickened and bubbly. Spoon over meat. Sprinkle with parsley and cheese. Makes 4 servings.

Low-calorie cooking tips

● Trim fat from steaks or chops, then panbroil without added fat in a skillet with Teflon or special nonstick coating. Or, brown the meat in a well-seasoned cast-iron skillet that has been generously sprinkled with salt.
● Poach fish in water or unsweetened fruit juices without added fat. Season with lemon juice or fresh herbs instead of butter or margarine.
● Make white sauce with little or no fat. Blend flour with a small amount of cold, skim milk; stir into remaining milk. Cook and stir till bubbly. Add a few drops yellow food coloring.

Shrimp Creole with Parsley Rice
(195 calories per serving)

  1 cup chopped onion
  1 cup chopped celery
  1 clove garlic, minced
  2 tablespoons shortening
  1 28-ounce can tomatoes
  1 15-ounce can tomato sauce
  2 tablespoons Worcestershire sauce
  2 teaspoons salt
  1 teaspoon sugar
  ½ teaspoon chili powder
     Dash bottled hot pepper sauce
  1 tablespoon cornstarch
  2 tablespoons cold water
1½ pounds fresh or frozen shelled shrimp
  1 cup chopped green pepper
  6 cups hot cooked rice
  ⅓ cup snipped parsley

In skillet cook onion, celery, and garlic in shortening till tender but not brown. (Electric skillet 300°.) Add tomatoes, tomato sauce, and next 5 ingredients. Reduce heat (220°). Simmer, uncovered, 45 minutes. Mix cornstarch with cold water; stir into sauce. Cook and stir till mixture thickens and bubbles. Add shrimp and green pepper. Cover; simmer 5 minutes. Combine rice and parsley. Serve shrimp mixture with the parsley rice. Makes 12 servings.

Curried Chicken
(285 calories per serving)

  3 whole chicken breasts (2½ pounds)
  3 chicken bouillon cubes
  ½ cup nonfat dry milk powder
  ¼ cup sliced green onions
  ¼ cup all-purpose flour
  1 tablespoon curry powder
  2 tablespoons chopped canned pimiento
  6 rusks
  1 hard-cooked egg, sliced
  2 tablespoons sliced green onion tops

Remove skin and bones from chicken; cut meat into cubes. Dissolve bouillon cubes in 2½ cups boiling water; cool. In skillet stir bouillon into dry milk powder. Add chicken and ¼ cup green onions. Simmer 10 minutes. (Electric skillet 220°.) Combine ¼ cup cold water, flour, curry powder, and ¼ teaspoon salt. Stir into chicken mixture with pimiento. Cook and stir till thickened. Serve over rusks. Trim with egg and onion tops. Serves 6.

Fruited Ham Slice
(245 calories per serving)

  1 fully cooked ham slice, cut 1 inch
     thick (2 pounds)
  1 16-ounce can apricot halves (juice
     pack)
  ½ cup low-calorie orange marmalade
  1 teaspoon finely chopped candied
     ginger
  1 cup seedless green grapes, halved
  1 tablespoon cornstarch

Trim excess fat from ham; slash edges at 1-inch intervals. Panbroil ham in heavy skillet over medium heat until lightly browned and heated, about 16 to 18 minutes, turning occasionally. (Electric skillet 300°.) Drain apricots, reserving juice. Combine juice with marmalade and ginger; pour around ham. Arrange apricots and grapes around ham. Reduce heat. Simmer, covered, to heat fruit, 5 minutes.

   Remove ham to heated platter; keep warm. Combine cornstarch and 2 tablespoons cold water; add to skillet mixture. Cook and stir till thickened and bubbly. Spoon some sauce over ham; pass remaining sauce. Serves 8.

TIME-WORTHY FAVORITES

Count on your heavy-duty and electric skillets when preparing less tender cuts of meat or chicken dishes, which benefit from a long, slow simmering. Place a tight-fitting cover on the skillet to keep the steam and juices in the pan during cooking. The meat becomes fork tender while the seasonings mingle deliciously.

The first part of this section features tasty pot roasts, stews, flank steaks, round steaks, and short ribs—all dishes that require an hour or more cooking time. They are handy dinners-in-a-skillet that simmer gently at a low heat setting while you work around the house.

Chicken recipes are the center of attention in the later part of the section. These take a little less time and a little more pot watching. Several are fried chicken variations; the remainder are cooked with vegetables or herbs.

Swedish Pot Roast

 1 3- to 4-pound beef chuck roast
 1 teaspoon salt
 4 whole cloves
 2 medium onions, quartered
 1 cup chopped carrots
 ½ cup chopped celery
 ⅓ cup water
 1 tablespoon corn syrup
 3 anchovy fillets
 2 tablespoons all-purpose flour
 ¼ cup cold water
   Salt and pepper

Trim excess fat from roast. Sprinkle salt into skillet. Brown the meat slowly on both sides. (Electric skillet 350°.) Cover skillet; reduce heat (220°). Stick cloves in onions. Add to meat along with carrots, celery, ⅓ cup water, corn syrup, and anchovies. Cover and simmer till meat is tender, about 2½ hours.

Remove meat to heated platter; keep warm. Skim excess fat from pan juices. Blend flour with ¼ cup water; stir into pan juices, mashing up the carrot and onion, if desired. Cook and stir until thickened and bubbly. Season with salt and pepper. Serve with roast. Serves 6 to 8.

Polynesian Pot Roast

 1 3-pound beef pot roast
 2 tablespoons cooking oil
   Salt
 ¼ cup flaked coconut
 ¼ cup pineapple-apricot preserves
 ¼ cup water
 1 tablespoon vinegar
 1 tablespoon soy sauce
 ½ teaspoon ground ginger
 ½ teaspoon grated lemon peel
   Dash pepper
         • • •
 4 teaspoons cornstarch
 2 tablespoons cold water
   Pineapple rings
   Watercress or parsley
   Hot cooked rice

In 12-inch skillet brown the pot roast slowly in hot oil. (Electric skillet 350°.) Sprinkle meat with a little salt. Combine flaked coconut, pineapple-apricot preserves, the ¼ cup water, vinegar, soy sauce, ginger, lemon peel, and pepper. Pour mixture over meat. Cover skillet tightly; reduce heat (220°). Simmer till meat is tender, 2 to 2¼ hours. Add water during cooking, if necessary.

Remove meat to heated platter; keep warm. Skim fat from pan juices. Measure pan juices; add water to make 1 cup. Return pan juices to skillet. Blend together cornstarch and the 2 tablespoons cold water; add to pan juices. Cook and stir over low heat till thickened and bubbly. Spoon some sauce over meat; pass the remainder with roast. Garnish meat with pineapple rings and watercress or parsley. Serve with hot cooked rice. Makes 6 to 8 servings.

Beef with a Scandinavian flair

Swedish Pot Roast *owes its well-seasoned goodness* → *to the anchovies and clove-studded onions cooked with the meat. Carrots and celery may be mashed in the gravy or left in pieces to add flecks of color.*

Convenient canned tamales are the surprise stuffing in Mexican Flank Steak, *which is tenderized by pounding, then rolled around the tamales.*

Cheesy Onion Steak

Have meatman cut a ½-inch-thick slice from a large roast to provide two meals from the same roast—

    ½ pound beef chuck steak, ½ inch thick
    2 tablespoons all-purpose flour
    ½ teaspoon salt
    2 tablespoons cooking oil
    4 slices onion
      Lemon pepper
    ¼ cup shredded process American cheese

Remove any bone from steak; cut meat in two pieces; coat with mixture of flour and salt. Pound to ¼-inch thickness. In 8-inch skillet brown the meat slowly in hot oil. Top each piece with two onion slices; sprinkle with lemon pepper. Add ½ cup water. Reduce heat; cover and simmer till tender, about 45 minutes. Sprinkle cheese over onion. Cover; heat 1 to 2 minutes to melt cheese. Makes 2 servings.

Mexican Flank Steak

    2 beef flank steaks, scored
        (1 pound each)
    ¾ teaspoon salt
    ⅛ teaspoon garlic salt
    ⅛ teaspoon pepper
    1 15-ounce can tamales in sauce
    2 tablespoons cooking oil
    1¼ cups boiling water
    1 8-ounce can tomato sauce (1 cup)
      Dash bottled hot pepper sauce

Pound meat well on both sides; sprinkle with salt, garlic salt, and pepper. Unwrap tamales; place in center of steaks, and roll as for a jelly roll. Brown the rolls in hot oil in a heavy skillet. (Electric skillet 350°.) Drain excess fat. Combine remaining ingredients. Pour over meat. Reduce heat. Cover; simmer till tender, basting occasionally, 1½ to 1¾ hours. Before serving, skim off fat. Makes 6 to 8 servings.

Gypsy Round Steak

    1½ pounds beef round steak, ½ inch thick
    2 tablespoons cooking oil
    1 large onion, sliced (1 cup)
    1 clove garlic, crushed
    1 teaspoon salt
    ¼ teaspoon cayenne pepper
    ⅛ teaspoon pepper
    2 teaspoons sesame seed
    1 cup sliced celery (½-inch slices)
    1 cup sliced carrots (½-inch slices)
    3 medium potatoes, peeled and quartered
    ⅓ cup pimiento-stuffed green olives,
        halved
    1 teaspoon cornstarch

Pound round steak to ¼-inch thickness; cut into 6 pieces. In skillet brown the steak in hot oil. (Electric skillet 350°.) Remove meat. In same skillet cook onion and garlic till tender. Stir in seasonings and *1 teaspoon* sesame seed. Return meat to skillet. Add ½ cup water.

Cover; reduce heat (220°). Simmer 30 minutes. Add vegetables and ½ cup water. Cover; simmer till vegetables are done, 30 minutes. Add olives; heat. Combine cornstarch and 1 teaspoon cold water; add to skillet. Cook and stir till bubbly. Top with sesame. Serves 6.

Round Steak Italiano

2 pounds beef round steak, ¾ inch thick
   Cooking oil
8 ounces bulk Italian sausage
1 8-ounce can tomato sauce (1 cup)
¾ cup apple juice
½ cup chopped onion
½ teaspoon garlic salt
¼ teaspoon dried oregano leaves,
   crushed
⅛ teaspoon pepper
   Hot buttered noodles
   Grated Parmesan cheese

Cut steak into 8 servings; pound to ½-inch thickness. In skillet brown the steaks in small amount of oil. (Electric skillet 350°.) Remove meat. In same skillet brown the sausage, breaking into small pieces. Drain off excess fat. Add next 6 ingredients to sausage. Return steak to skillet. Reduce heat (220°); cover and simmer 50 to 60 minutes. Serve over hot, buttered noodles; pass grated Parmesan cheese. Serves 8.

Beef Roll-Ups with Spinach

2 pounds beef round steak, ¼ inch thick
1 clove garlic, halved
½ pound fresh spinach, cooked and
   drained (1 cup cooked)
¾ cup soft bread crumbs, toasted
½ cup grated Parmesan cheese
½ teaspoon dried sage leaves, crushed
½ teaspoon dried thyme leaves, crushed
2 tablespoons cooking oil
½ cup dry red wine
1 tablespoon all-purpose flour

Pound meat till very thin; cut in 8 pieces. Rub with cut garlic; season with salt and pepper. Combine spinach, crumbs, cheese, sage, and thyme; mound ¼ cup on each piece of meat. Roll up; tie with string. In heavy skillet brown the meat in hot oil. (Electric skillet 350°.) Reduce heat. Add wine and ¼ cup water.

Cover; simmer till meat is tender, about 30 minutes. Turn occasionally; add water, if needed. Transfer meat to platter; keep warm. Remove strings. Mix flour in 2 tablespoons cold water; stir into pan juices. Cook and stir till thick and bubbly. Pour over meat. Serves 6 to 8.

Spicy Orange Pot Roast

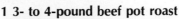

1 3- to 4-pound beef pot roast
1 tablespoon all-purpose flour
1 teaspoon salt
¼ teaspoon pepper
2 tablespoons shortening
1 teaspoon grated orange peel
½ cup orange juice
¼ cup brown sugar
½ teaspoon ground nutmeg
¼ teaspoon dried thyme leaves, crushed
1 orange, peeled and sliced
2 tablespoons cornstarch

Coat roast with mixture of flour, salt, and pepper. In large skillet brown the meat on all sides in hot shortening. (Electric skillet 350°.) Pour off excess fat. Combine next 5 ingredients; pour over meat. Cover; reduce heat (220°). Simmer till meat is tender, 2 to 2½ hours. Add water during cooking, if needed.

Cut orange slices in half; add to skillet. Cover; cook just to heat oranges, about 5 minutes. Remove roast to platter; keep warm. Blend cornstarch and 2 tablespoons cold water; stir into pan juices. Cook and stir till thickened and bubbly. Serve with roast. Serves 6 to 8.

Electric Skillet Veal Roast

Use your electric skillet as a mini oven—

3 tablespoons butter, softened
1 tablespoon dried onion flakes
2 cloves garlic, crushed
1 tablespoon lemon juice
1 teaspoon salt
¼ teaspoon dried dillweed, crushed
   Dash freshly ground pepper
1 3-pound rolled veal shoulder roast

Blend first 7 ingredients; spread over top and sides of roast. Place meat in center of large piece of heavy-duty foil; bring top edges together lengthwise, and fold over twice to make a firm seal. Fold over each end to seal. Place on rack in electric skillet preheated to 400° with vent open. Roast to 170° on meat thermometer, about 2 hours. Open foil; skim fat from juices. Remove strings; slice meat. Spoon juices over each serving. Makes 8 servings.

Veal Stew

3 pounds lean boneless veal, cubed
3 tablespoons cooking oil
2 tablespoons all-purpose flour
1 teaspoon salt
Dash freshly ground pepper
1½ cups dry white wine
½ cup chopped onion
¼ teaspoon dried thyme leaves
3 or 4 sprigs parsley
1 bay leaf
1 clove garlic, halved
1 cup light cream
2 beaten egg yolks
1 tablespoon snipped parsley

In large, heavy skillet lightly brown the veal in oil. (Electric skillet 350°.) Reduce heat (220°). Pour off fat. Stir in flour, salt, and pepper. Add wine and ½ cup water. Tie next 5 ingredients together in cheesecloth bag; add to skillet. Cover. Simmer till meat is tender, 50 to 60 minutes. Remove bag; discard. Beat cream into egg yolks; stir into pan juices. Cook and stir till thickened, 3 to 5 minutes. Sprinkle with parsley. Makes 6 servings.

Pork and Vegetable Medley

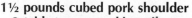

1½ pounds cubed pork shoulder
2 tablespoons cooking oil
½ cup chopped onion
1 cup sliced celery (½-inch slices)
1 3-ounce can mushrooms, undrained
1 15-ounce can tomato sauce
2 cups water
⅓ cup catsup
1 teaspoon salt
½ teaspoon garlic salt
¼ teaspoon dried basil leaves, crushed
¼ teaspoon pepper
1 10-ounce package frozen lima beans
4 ounces uncooked medium noodles

In large skillet brown the pork in oil. (Electric skillet 350°.) Push meat to one side. In same skillet cook onion till tender but not brown. Spoon off excess fat. Stir in remaining ingredients. Bring to boiling. Reduce heat (220°). Cover and simmer, stirring occasionally, till meat is tender, about 30 minutes. Makes 6 servings.

Lamb-Lentil Stew

1 pound cubed lamb shoulder
2 tablespoons cooking oil
1½ cups chopped onion
1 cup cut-up celery
3 chicken bouillon cubes
3 cloves garlic, minced
2 bay leaves
½ teaspoon dried oregano leaves, crushed
½ teaspoon salt
Dash pepper
1 cup dried lentils
4 medium carrots, cut up

In large skillet brown the meat in hot oil. (Electric skillet 350°.) Pour off excess fat. Add next 8 ingredients and 3 cups water. Reduce heat (220°). Cover and simmer 1 hour. Rinse lentils in cold water; drain. Add to lamb with carrots and 2½ cups water. Cover; simmer till tender, stirring once or twice, about 1 hour. Add water, if needed. Remove bay leaves. Serves 4.

Continental Beef and Rice

1½ pounds boneless beef chuck, cut in 1-inch cubes
3 tablespoons cooking oil
1½ teaspoons salt
¼ teaspoon pepper
¾ cup chopped onion
1 clove garlic, crushed
1 16-ounce can tomatoes, cut up
¾ cup water
½ cup dry red wine
2 tablespoons snipped parsley
1 teaspoon sugar
½ teaspoon dried thyme leaves, crushed
3 tablespoons all-purpose flour
Hot cooked rice

In large skillet brown the meat on all sides in hot oil. (Electric skillet 350°.) Season with salt and pepper. Push meat to one side. Cook onion and garlic; drain off excess fat. Reduce heat (220°). Add next 6 ingredients. Cover; simmer till meat is tender, about 1 hour. Combine flour and ⅓ cup cold water; add to skillet. Cook and stir till thickened and bubbly. Spoon beef mixture over hot cooked rice. Serves 6.

Braise to tenderize meat

● A tightly covered skillet, slow cooking, and liquid in the form of water or a seasoned sauce will make less-tender cuts of meat fork tender.

● Brown the meat at high heat (electric skillet 350° to 400°). Add seasonings and liquid. Cover skillet tightly. Close vent on electric skillet.

● Reduce heat to simmer (electric skillet 220° to 250°). Maintain gentlest boil possible. If mixture bubbles too hard, liquid evaporates quickly and will boil dry. Check mixture occasionally; add water, if needed.

Beef Stew with Potato Dumplings

  2 tablespoons all-purpose flour
  ½ teaspoon salt
  ⅛ teaspoon pepper
1½ pounds beef stew meat
  2 onions, sliced
  2 tablespoons bacon drippings
  1 10½-ounce can condensed beef broth
  1 tablespoon vinegar
  3 medium carrots, sliced ½ inch thick
     ● ● ●
    Potato Dumplings
    Snipped parsley

Combine flour, salt, and pepper; coat meat. In large skillet cook meat and onions in bacon drippings till meat is brown and onion is tender. (Electric skillet 350°.) Stir in broth, ¾ cup water, and vinegar; add carrots. Bring to boiling; reduce heat (220°). Cover and simmer till tender, 1½ hours. Drop Potato Dumplings onto bubbling stew; cover and simmer 15 minutes. Sprinkle with parsley. Makes 5 servings.

Potato Dumplings: Combine 1 beaten egg, ¾ cup soft bread crumbs, 1 tablespoon all-purpose flour, 1 tablespoon finely chopped onion, 1 tablespoon snipped parsley, ½ teaspoon salt, and dash pepper. Stir in 2½ cups finely shredded raw potato. With floured fingers, form potato mixture in ten 2-inch balls. Dust lightly with flour before dropping onto stew.

Short Ribs with Limas

  3 pounds beef short ribs, cut in serving-sized pieces
1½ teaspoons salt
  ⅛ teaspoon pepper
1½ cups water
  ¾ cup brown sugar
  ½ cup chopped onion
  ⅓ cup vinegar
1½ teaspoons dry mustard
  2 bay leaves
  2 teaspoons cornstarch
  2 16-ounce cans cooked, dried lima beans, drained

Trim excess fat from short ribs; cook trimmings in skillet till 2 tablespoons fat accumulate. (Electric skillet 350°.) Discard trimmings. Brown the ribs on all sides. Drain off excess fat. Reduce heat (220°). Sprinkle ribs with salt and pepper. Add next 6 ingredients. Cover; simmer till ribs are tender, about 2 hours. Discard bay leaves. Remove ribs; keep hot. Spoon off fat. Blend cornstarch with ¼ cup cold water. Add to meat juices; cook and stir till thickened and bubbly. Add beans. Cover; simmer 5 to 10 minutes. Serve with short ribs. Serves 6.

Lamb-Stuffed Cabbage Leaves

10 large cabbage leaves
  1 pound ground lamb
  ½ cup chopped onion
  ½ cup uncooked packaged precooked rice
  1 tablespoon chopped fresh mint
  1 teaspoon salt
    Dash pepper
  1 cup water
  2 tablespoons lemon juice
    Plain yogurt

Soften cabbage leaves by immersing in boiling water till limp, about 3 minutes; drain. Combine lamb, onion, rice, mint, salt, and pepper. Place about ¼ cup meat mixture in center of each cabbage leaf. Fold in sides and roll ends over meat. Fasten with wooden picks, if desired. Place in large skillet; add water and lemon juice. Bring to boiling. (Electric skillet 350°.) Reduce heat (220°); simmer, covered, 1 hour. Serve hot. Pass yogurt. Makes 5 servings.

Chicken and Potato Paprika

1 2½- to 3-pound ready-to-cook
    broiler-fryer chicken, cut up
2 tablespoons butter
1 tablespoon paprika
1 chicken bouillon cube
½ cup dry white wine
½ cup chopped onion
1 teaspoon salt
  Dash pepper
4 medium potatoes, peeled and quartered
1 medium green pepper, finely chopped
1 tablespoon all-purpose flour
1 cup dairy sour cream

In 12-inch skillet brown the chicken pieces in butter. (Electric skillet 350°.) Sprinkle with paprika. Dissolve bouillon cube in ¾ cup water; pour over chicken. Add wine, onion, ½ *teaspoon* of the salt, and pepper. Cover and reduce heat (220°); simmer 15 minutes. Add potatoes and green pepper to skillet. Sprinkle remaining ½ teaspoon salt over all. Cover; simmer till chicken and potatoes are tender, 30 minutes.

Place chicken and potatoes on platter; keep warm. Stir flour into sour cream; stir in ¼ cup pan liquid. Slowly add sour cream mixture to liquid in skillet. Cook and stir over low heat till heated through. Spoon over chicken and potatoes. Makes 4 servings.

When frying chicken, turn the meat with tongs to retain the juices and to protect yourself from spatters. Brown the meatier parts first, then remainder.

Lemon Chicken

Pictured on page 2—

⅓ cup all-purpose flour
1 teaspoon paprika
1 2½- to 3-pound ready-to-cook
    broiler-fryer chicken, cut up
3 tablespoons lemon juice
3 tablespoons shortening
1 chicken bouillon cube
¼ cup thinly sliced green onion
2 tablespoons brown sugar
1½ teaspoons grated lemon peel
2 tablespoons snipped parsley

Combine flour, 1 teaspoon salt, and paprika in paper or plastic bag. Brush chicken with lemon juice. Add 2 or 3 pieces of chicken at a time to bag and shake well. In 12-inch skillet brown the chicken slowly in hot shortening. (Electric skillet 350°.) Dissolve bouillon cube in ¾ cup boiling water; pour over chicken. Stir in green onion, brown sugar, lemon peel, and any remaining lemon juice. Cover; reduce heat (220°). Cook over low heat till chicken is tender, 40 to 45 minutes. Sprinkle with parsley. Makes 4 servings.

Deviled Chicken

⅓ cup all-purpose flour
½ teaspoon pepper
½ teaspoon garlic salt
½ teaspoon dry mustard
½ teaspoon paprika
¼ teaspoon cayenne
1 2½- to 3-pound ready-to-cook
    broiler-fryer chicken, cut up
3 tablespoons shortening
1 chicken bouillon cube
½ cup chili sauce
2 tablespoons lemon juice

Combine first 6 ingredients and ½ teaspoon salt in paper or plastic bag; add 2 or 3 pieces of chicken at a time to bag and shake well. In 12-inch skillet brown the chicken slowly in hot shortening. (Electric skillet 350°.) Reduce heat (220°). Dissolve bouillon cube in 1 cup boiling water. Stir in last two ingredients; add to skillet. Cover and simmer 40 minutes. Makes 4 servings.

Three things spell success in browning Batter-Fried Chicken: *Before adding chicken, have oil hot enough that a drop of water sizzles (prevents greasiness); do few pieces at a time; and use a heavy skillet.*

Batter-Fried Chicken

- 1 2- to 2½-pound ready-to-cook broiler-fryer chicken, cut up
- 1 cup pancake mix
- ½ teaspoon salt
- ¾ cup water
- Cooking oil

Simmer chicken in salted water for 20 minutes; drain. Combine pancake mix and salt; stir in water. Beat 2 minutes. Dip chicken in batter; drain well on rack over waxed paper. In heavy skillet at least 3 inches deep, heat oil 1¼ inches deep to 350°. (Electric skillet, see tip, page 72.) Regulate heat so chicken fries at about 325°. Fry a few pieces at a time till golden, about 5 minutes. Drain. Makes 4 servings.

Favorite Fried Chicken

- ⅓ cup all-purpose flour
- 1 teaspoon salt
- 1 teaspoon paprika
- ¼ teaspoon pepper
- 1 2½- to 3-pound ready-to-cook broiler-fryer chicken, cut up
- Cooking oil

Combine flour, salt, paprika, and pepper in paper or plastic bag. Add 2 or 3 pieces of chicken at a time; shake well. Dry on rack. Heat oil ¼ inch deep in 12-inch skillet. (Electric skillet 350°.) Brown the chicken slowly, turning with tongs. Reduce heat (220°); cover tightly and cook till tender, 30 to 40 minutes. Uncover last 10 minutes. Serves 4.

Regional American Recipes

Take a culinary journey across the USA by sampling good regional foods that are still cooked in a skillet today. Note the blending of local foods and the influence of settlers of differing nationalities.

New England and Northeast dishes benefit from the thrifty hands and seasoning art of the Pilgrims, the Pennsylvania Dutch, and the Shakers. Down in the South and Southeast, amid traditions of gracious dining, the French and Creole culinary touches emerge.

Hardy pioneers of many lands turned the prairie into farms and fished the lakes of the Midwest and mountain states.

Foods with a Spanish heritage appear at a barbecue in the Southwest, while oriental dishes team with vegetables and fruits in the varied cuisine of the West Coast and Hawaii.

The Midwestern states produce lean, tender pork, and up in Minnesota wild rice is harvested. The foods combine handsomely in the *Pork Chop and Wild Rice Skillet* on page 54.

NEW ENGLAND AND NORTHEAST

The Pilgrims established more than Thanksgiving from the first year's harvest of corn, beans, and pumpkin at Plimoth Plantation. They proved that people could feed themselves in a new land.

From the Indians they learned to grind corn for meal, to tap maple trees for syrup, to fish for cod, and to tread out clams from the tidal flats of Cape Cod, food customs that became established as their descendants moved west.

Later groups leaving Europe—the English Quakers and the Germans for Pennsylvania, the Shakers for New York—also learned survival in the wilderness from the Indians, mainly how to use maize. Pennsylvanians not only baked with cornmeal, they mixed it with pork scraps on butchering day for scrapple. This recipe, along with other pioneer skillet recipes, is included on the following pages.

Johnnycakes (or Journeycakes)

Here's an electric skillet version of the cornmeal cakes that the Pilgrims carried on journeys—

    1 beaten egg
 1½ cups milk
    1 tablespoon cooking oil
    1 teaspoon salt
    2 cups yellow or white cornmeal
      Butter or margarine
      Warm syrup

Combine egg, milk, oil, salt, and cornmeal; mix well. Drop scant ¼ cup of batter into well-greased, hot skillet, spreading ¼ inch thick. (Electric skillet 350°.) Cook over medium heat till golden brown, 2 or 3 minutes per side. Serve warm with butter and syrup. Makes 10.

Cranberry Sauce

Combine 2 cups *each* sugar and water in large skillet; stir to dissolve sugar. Heat to boiling; boil 5 minutes. (Electric skillet 250°.) Add 1 pound fresh cranberries; cook till skins pop, 5 minutes. Remove from heat. Makes 4 cups.

Yankee Red-Flannel Hash

 ⅓ cup finely chopped onion
 ¼ cup hot shortening
    3 cups diced, peeled, cooked potatoes
    1 16-ounce can beets, drained and diced
 1½ cups diced, cooked corned beef
 ⅓ cup milk
 ½ teaspoon salt
    1 or 2 drops bottled hot pepper sauce

In skillet cook onion in shortening till tender but not brown. (Electric skillet 300°.) Toss with remaining ingredients; spread evenly in skillet. Cover and cook over medium heat till brown and crusty. Makes 4 servings.

Funnel Cakes

    2 beaten eggs
 1½ cups milk
    2 cups sifted all-purpose flour
    1 teaspoon baking powder
 ½ teaspoon salt
    2 cups cooking oil
      Sifted powdered sugar

In mixing bowl combine eggs and milk. Sift together flour, baking powder, and salt. Add to egg mixture; beat smooth. In deep skillet heat oil to 360°. (Electric skillet, see tip, page 72.) Covering spout with finger, pour ¼ cup batter into funnel. Remove finger and release batter into oil in a spiral, starting in center and winding out. Fry till golden, about 3 minutes. Turn carefully; cook 1 minute more. Drain on paper toweling; dust with powdered sugar. Makes 6 to 8 funnel cakes.

Pennsylvania Dutch brunch

Funnel Cakes are shaped by pouring batter through → a funnel into hot oil in a spiral. The finished cakes are dusted with powdered sugar and served with maple syrup and sausages for breakfast.

Shaker-Style Steak

This fine way to tenderize beef round steak is courtesy of a religious sect who like things plain and simple, furniture as well as food—

> 2 pounds beef round steak
> ¼ cup all-purpose flour
> Salt
> Pepper
> ¾ cup finely chopped onion
> ¾ cup finely chopped carrot
> ½ cup finely chopped celery
> ¼ cup finely chopped green pepper
> ¾ cup catsup
> ¾ cup water
> 1 tablespoon vinegar

Trim fat from steak; cook trimmings in skillet till 2 tablespoons drippings accumulate. (Electric skillet 350°.) Pound flour into steak with meat mallet. Brown in hot drippings; spoon off excess fat. Season with salt and pepper. Combine onion, carrot, celery, green pepper, catsup, water, and vinegar. Pour over and around meat. Reduce heat (220°). Cover skillet and simmer till meat is tender and vegetables are cooked, about 1 hour. Serve with sauce. Makes 6 to 8 servings.

Codfish Cakes

> 1 pound salt cod
> 5 medium potatoes, peeled
>   and diced (5 cups)
> 2 eggs
> 2 tablespoons butter, softened
> 2 teaspoons prepared mustard
> 1 teaspoon Worcestershire sauce
> ¼ teaspoon pepper
> 2 tablespoons cooking oil

Soak cod in cold water 8 hours or overnight; change water twice. Dice cod (should be 3 cups). Cook cod and potatoes in boiling water till potatoes are tender, about 10 to 15 minutes; drain. Beat with electric mixer. Add eggs, butter, mustard, Worcestershire, and pepper; beat well. Using ⅓ cup mixture for each, shape into ½-inch patties. In skillet cook patties in hot oil till crisp and brown, 2 to 3 minutes, turning once. (Electric skillet 350°.) Serves 6 to 8.

Maple-Nut Dumplings

Yankee women used a seasoned spider, a black iron skillet with three legs, to make this dessert—

> 1½ cups maple-flavored syrup
> 1 cup water
> 1 teaspoon vanilla
> 1½ cups sifted all-purpose flour
> ⅓ cup sugar
> 1 tablespoon baking powder
> ½ teaspoon salt
> ⅔ cup milk
> 2 tablespoons cooking oil
> ¼ cup coarsely chopped walnuts

In skillet combine maple syrup, water, and vanilla; bring to boiling. (Electric skillet 350°.) In mixing bowl sift together flour, sugar, baking powder, and salt. Stir in milk and oil. Drop onto boiling syrup in 6 portions. Sprinkle with nuts. Reduce heat. (Electric skillet 220°.) Cover and simmer till done, 10 to 12 minutes. Serve warm. Makes 6 servings.

Pennsylvania Dutch Pork Chops

Settlers from southern Germany developed a hearty style of cooking that matched the abundance of their large, well-kept farms in the Allegheny foothills—

> 4 shoulder pork chops, cut
>   ½ inch thick (2 pounds)
> 1 8-ounce can applesauce
> 1 16-ounce can sauerkraut, undrained
>   and snipped
> ¼ cup finely chopped onion
> 2 tablespoons brown sugar
> ¾ teaspoon caraway seed

Trim excess fat from chops; cook trimmings in skillet till 1 tablespoon fat accumulates. (Electric skillet 300°.) Discard trimmings. Brown the chops slowly on both sides in hot fat. Remove chops; drain off fat. Reduce heat (220°). Reserve ¼ cup applesauce. Combine remaining applesauce with sauerkraut, onion, brown sugar, and caraway seed; add to skillet. Add chops; season with salt and pepper. Spoon dollop of reserved applesauce over each chop. Cover and simmer till chops are tender, 35 to 45 minutes. Makes 4 servings.

Red Cabbage and Apples

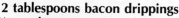

2 tablespoons bacon drippings
¼ cup brown sugar
¼ cup vinegar
¼ cup water
½ teaspoon salt
Dash pepper
4 to 5 whole cloves
1 small onion, peeled
½ medium head red cabbage, shredded
(4 cups)
2 cups peeled, sliced apples

In a medium skillet heat the bacon drippings. (Electric skillet 350°.) Blend in brown sugar, vinegar, water, salt, and pepper. Insert the whole cloves into onion. Add onion, shredded cabbage, and sliced apple to skillet. Cover; reduce heat (220°). Cook, stirring occasionally, till cabbage is tender, 25 to 30 minutes. Remove the onion. Makes 6 servings.

New England Fish Chowder

Along the old Boston post road, inns welcomed stage-coach passengers with steaming bowls of fish chowder, still a fine warm-up on a cold day—

¼ cup butter or margarine
1 large onion, thinly sliced
1 pound fresh or frozen
haddock, skinned, boned, and cubed
4 cups cubed, peeled potatoes
2 cups water
2 tablespoons all-purpose flour
2 cups milk
¾ teaspoon salt
Dash freshly ground pepper
Dash paprika
Oyster crackers

Melt *2 tablespoons* of the butter in heavy skillet. (Electric skillet 300°.) Add onion and cook till tender. Arrange fish and potatoes in layers in skillet; add water. Cover and cook gently (220°) till potatoes are barely tender, about 15 minutes. Blend remaining butter and flour; mix in a little of the hot fish liquor. Stir into fish mixture; cook till slightly thickened. Add milk, salt, pepper, and paprika. Simmer 5 minutes. Serve with oyster crackers. Makes 6 servings.

Scrapple

Serve with scrambled eggs and applesauce—

1 pound bulk pork sausage
3 chicken bouillon cubes
3½ cups boiling water
1 cup yellow cornmeal
¼ teaspoon salt
⅛ teaspoon dried thyme leaves, crushed
Dash ground cloves

• • •

All-purpose flour
1 beaten egg
2 tablespoons milk
Shortening
Warm maple syrup
Butter or margarine

In skillet brown the sausage slowly, stirring to break into small pieces; drain off fat. (Electric skillet 350°.) Dissolve bouillon cubes in boiling water; add to sausage. Bring to boiling. Slowly stir in cornmeal, salt, thyme, and cloves. Cook 5 minutes, stirring constantly. Pour into greased 8½x4½x2½-inch loaf dish. Chill till firm. Unmold and cut in ½-inch slices. Dip in flour, then in a mixture of egg and milk, and again in flour. In skillet slowly brown in hot shortening 8 to 10 minutes on each side. Serve with syrup and butter. Makes 6 servings.

Maine Blueberry Pancakes

1½ cups fresh blueberries
1½ cups sifted all-purpose flour
3 tablespoons sugar
2 tablespoons baking powder
½ teaspoon salt
2 beaten eggs
1¼ cups milk
3 tablespoons cooking oil
Cooking oil for frying

Wash blueberries; drain very thoroughly. Sift together flour, sugar, baking powder, and salt. Combine eggs, milk, and oil; add dry ingredients. Beat till smooth. Gently fold in drained berries. Bake pancakes in hot, lightly greased skillet. (Electric skillet 375°.) Cook till tops are covered with tiny bubbles; turn and brown on other side. Makes 14 four-inch pancakes.

SOUTH AND SOUTHEAST

The South is pork, ham, chicken, and seafood country. Clams, oysters, and shrimp are eaten along the coast, and fish are panfried inland along the rivers. Rice, sweet potatoes, and corn — as grits, hominy, or meal — are the South's starches. Peas, butter beans, collards, and okra are some of the favorite green vegetables.

From Maryland's Mason-Dixon line through the tidewater of Virginia and the Carolinas to Georgia, the cooking influence is chiefly English. From Florida around the Gulf to Louisiana, it's Spanish and French, while liberal Creole seasonings give New Orleans a style all its own.

Maryland Fried Chicken

1 beaten egg
1¼ cups milk
⅔ cup fine cracker crumbs
1 2½- to 3-pound ready-to-cook
    broiler-fryer chicken, cut up
3 to 4 tablespoons shortening

Combine egg and ¼ *cup* of the milk. Mix cracker crumbs with ½ teaspoon salt and dash pepper. Dip chicken pieces into egg mixture; roll in crumbs. Heat shortening in heavy 12-inch skillet. (Electric skillet 350°.) Brown the chicken pieces slowly, turning with tongs. Add remaining 1 cup milk. Reduce heat (220°); cover tightly and simmer 35 minutes. Uncover; cook till tender, about 10 minutes more. From pan drippings, make Cream Gravy. Serves 4.

Cream Gravy

1½ cups milk
3 tablespoons all-purpose flour
3 tablespoons pan drippings

In a screw-top jar shake ¾ *cup* of the milk with flour, 1 teaspoon salt, and dash pepper till blended; stir into drippings in pan. Add remaining ¾ cup milk. Cook, stirring constantly, till thickened and bubbly. Cook 2 to 3 minutes longer. Makes 1½ cups.

Hush Puppies

While frying catfish, the cooks put some of the corn-meal coating into hot fat. They then tossed the results to the dogs to quiet them—

2 cups cornmeal
½ cup sifted all-purpose flour
1 tablespoon sugar
2 teaspoons baking powder
½ teaspoon baking soda
½ teaspoon salt
1 well-beaten egg
1 cup buttermilk
⅓ cup finely chopped onion
¼ cup water
    Cooking oil
    Butter or margarine

Combine cornmeal, flour, sugar, baking powder, soda, and salt. Combine egg, buttermilk, onion, and water; stir into cornmeal mixture just till moistened. In a skillet that is at least 3 inches deep, pour in oil to depth of 1½ inches. Heat oil to 375°. (Electric skillet, see tip, page 72.) Drop batter by tablespoonfuls into hot oil. Fry till golden brown, turning once, about 2 minutes. Drain on paper toweling. Serve hot with butter. Makes about 2 dozen hush puppies.

Peach-Glazed Sweet Potatoes

Georgia peaches, in the form of peach preserves, add sweetness to these potatoes—

½ cup peach preserves
¼ cup brown sugar
1 tablespoon lemon juice
¼ teaspoon ground cinnamon
4 medium sweet potatoes, cooked, peeled,
    and cut in 2-inch slices (2 pounds)

In skillet combine preserves, brown sugar, lemon juice, and cinnamon; heat till bubbly. (Electric skillet 350°.) Add sweet potatoes; cook and stir over low heat (220°) till heated through and glazed, 10 to 15 minutes. Serves 4 to 6.

In honor of the Derby, serve juleps with brunch. The traditional Ham With Red-Eye Gravy features lean, dry-salt, smoke-cured, country-style ham. Bits that cling to skillet are 'red eyes' in the drippings served with grits.

Ham with Red-Eye Gravy

3 country ham or fully cooked ham slices, cut ½ inch thick
⅔ cup boiling water
1 teaspoon instant coffee powder
Liquid smoke (optional)

Cut ham slice in half. Trim fat from ham, reserving trimmings. In skillet cook trimmings till crisp. (Electric skillet 350°.) Discard trimmings and brown the ham on both sides in hot fat, 5 to 6 minutes per side. Remove ham to warm platter. Stir boiling water and coffee powder into drippings. Add liquid smoke if ham is mild-cured. Cook, scraping pan to remove crusty bits, for 2 or 3 minutes. Serve over ham, and with grits, if desired. Makes 6 servings.

Spicy Sugared Pecans

These sugary confections are easy to make—the pumpkin pie spice saves measuring three spices—

¾ cup sugar
¼ cup water
¾ teaspoon pumpkin pie spice
2 cups pecan or walnut halves

In skillet combine sugar, water, and pumpkin pie spice. (Electric skillet 250°.) Bring mixture to a full rolling boil; boil till sugar crystals form on sides of skillet, 5 to 6 minutes (3 minutes with electric skillet). Add pecan or walnut halves; stir till nuts are sugar-coated. Turn out onto waxed paper or foil. Quickly separate nuts, using two forks. Cool. Makes 2 cups.

Shrimp Gumbo

1 pound fresh or frozen shelled shrimp
½ cup chopped celery
½ cup chopped onion
2 cloves garlic, minced
2 tablespoons cooking oil
1 16-ounce can tomatoes, cut up
2 cups sliced, fresh okra, or 1 10-
    ounce package frozen, cut okra
1 teaspoon salt
¼ teaspoon pepper
2 bay leaves
   Dash bottled hot pepper sauce
½ cup water (optional)
   Hot cooked rice

Thaw frozen shrimp. In heavy skillet cook celery, onion, and garlic in hot oil till tender. (Electric skillet 300°.) Add tomatoes, okra, salt, pepper, bay leaves, and hot pepper sauce. Reduce heat (220°). Cover; simmer 10 minutes. Add shrimp; cook 10 to 15 minutes more. Remove bay leaves. If thinner consistency is desired, add ½ cup water; heat through. Serve in soup bowls with hot cooked rice. Serves 6.

Cooking celery, onion, and garlic in oil for Shrimp Gumbo *is called sautéing from a French verb that means to leap, as vegetables do in hot fat.*

Hopping John

8 ounces dry black-eyed peas
1½ cups chopped onion
½ teaspoon pepper
¼ teaspoon dried red pepper, crushed
1 large clove garlic, minced
1 bay leaf
8 ounces salt pork, rinsed and cut in
    12 pieces
   Hot cooked rice

Rinse peas; in skillet bring to boiling in 1 quart water. (Electric skillet 250°.) Boil 2 minutes; remove from heat and let stand 1 hour. Add onion, pepper, red pepper, garlic, and bay leaf. Bring to boiling; cover and reduce heat (220°). Simmer 1 hour, stirring once or twice. Stir in salt pork; simmer, uncovered, till tender, stirring frequently, 50 to 60 minutes more. Remove salt pork and bay leaf; mash the pea mixture slightly. Season to taste with additional salt, if desired. Serve with hot rice. Serves 4 to 6.

Cream-Sauced Frogs Legs

Frog hunting is known as gigging when done at the pond instead of at the supermarket—

2 pounds fresh or frozen frogs legs
⅓ cup all-purpose flour
1½ teaspoons salt
½ teaspoon dried tarragon leaves, crushed
¼ teaspoon pepper
¼ cup butter or margarine
2 tablespoons finely chopped onion
1½ cups light cream
2 tablespoons snipped parsley

Thaw frozen frogs legs. Separate into single legs. Combine flour, salt, tarragon, and pepper in paper or plastic bag; shake frogs legs a few at a time to coat well. Reserve remaining flour mixture. In large skillet brown the legs in butter. (Electric skillet 350°.) Cook, covered, till done, about 25 minutes. Remove frogs legs to platter; keep warm.

In same skillet cook onion till tender but not brown (300°). Blend in 1 tablespoon reserved flour mixture. Stir in cream; cook and stir till thickened and bubbly. Spoon over frogs legs. Garnish with parsley. Makes 6 servings.

French Doughnuts

      3 cups sifted all-purpose flour
      1 package active dry yeast
      ½ teaspoon ground nutmeg
      1 cup milk
      ¼ cup sugar
      ¼ cup cooking oil
      ¾ teaspoon salt
      1 egg
        Cooking oil
        Sifted powdered sugar

In large mixer bowl combine 1¾ *cups* of the flour, the yeast, and nutmeg. In saucepan heat milk, sugar, oil, and salt just till warm, stirring occasionally. Add to yeast mixture; add egg. Beat at low speed of electric mixer for ½ minute, scraping sides of bowl constantly. Beat 3 minutes at high speed. By hand, stir in enough of the remaining flour to make a soft dough. Turn into greased bowl; cover and chill.

Turn dough out onto well-floured surface; form into ball. Cover and let rest 10 minutes. Roll dough to an 18x12-inch rectangle. Cut in 3x2-inch rectangles. Cover and let rise 30 minutes. (Dough will not be doubled.) In skillet that is at least 3 inches deep, heat 1½ inches oil to 375°. (Electric skillet, see tip, page 72.) Fry a few doughnuts at a time, turning once, till golden, about 1 minute. Drain on paper toweling; sprinkle with powdered sugar. Makes 3 dozen doughnuts.

Pain Perdu (New Orleans French Toast)

      ⅔ cup milk
      2 beaten eggs
      2 tablespoons powdered sugar
      1 teaspoon grated lemon peel
      8 slices day-old French bread,
          1 inch thick
        Butter or margarine
        Powdered sugar
        Maple syrup or honey

Combine milk, eggs, sugar, lemon peel, and dash salt; mix well. Dip bread in egg mixture, coating both sides. In skillet over low heat, brown the bread in butter on both sides. (Electric skillet 275°.) Sprinkle with powdered sugar. Serve hot with butter and syrup. Serves 4.

New Orleans Calas (Rice Cakes)

      ⅓ cup long grain rice, cooked (1 cup)
      1 package active dry yeast
      ½ cup warm water
      3 well-beaten eggs
      1 cup sifted all-purpose flour
      ⅓ cup sugar
      ½ teaspoon salt
      ¼ teaspoon ground nutmeg
        Cooking oil
        Sifted powdered sugar

In mixing bowl mash rice; cool to lukewarm. Soften yeast in warm water; stir into rice. Mix well. Cover and let stand overnight. Add eggs, flour, sugar, salt, and nutmeg; beat well. Let stand in warm place for 30 minutes.

In skillet that is at least 3 inches deep, heat oil 1 inch deep to 375°. (Electric skillet, see tip, page 72.) Drop batter by tablespoons into hot oil; fry till golden brown, about 1 minute on each side. Drain on paper toweling. Dust with powdered sugar; serve warm. Makes 32.

Crawfish à la Creole

      2 tablespoons butter or margarine
      2 tablespoons all-purpose flour
      1 cup chopped onion
      ½ cup chopped green pepper
      2 tomatoes, chopped (2 cups)
      1 tablespoon snipped parsley
      2 cloves garlic, minced
      ¾ teaspoon salt
      ½ teaspoon dried thyme leaves, crushed
      1 bay leaf
      6 pounds live crawfish, cooked and
          shelled (1 pound meat), or 1 pound
          cooked, shelled shrimp
        Bottled hot pepper sauce
                • • •
        Hot cooked rice

In skillet melt butter; blend in flour and cook till lightly browned. (Electric skillet 250°.) Add onion and green pepper; cook till tender but not brown. Add tomatoes, parsley, garlic, salt, thyme, bay leaf, and ¼ cup water. Cover and simmer 45 minutes. Stir in crawfish and heat through, about 10 minutes. Season with hot pepper sauce. Serve over rice. Serves 4.

MIDWEST AND MOUNTAIN

Many Scandinavian and German settlers plowed the prairie between Ohio and the Dakotas, planting corn and wheat in the fertile soil. They left a strong imprint on food patterns. Pork is a favored meat, potatoes and cabbage are popular vegetables, and cardamom and cinnamon are the preferred spices for baking.

Home was first a covered wagon; then a sod house or log cabin. Glass window panes were a luxury. A resourceful pioneer woman had many ways of making do. For instance, she scrambled not-so-fresh eggs with wild onion to mask the flavor—thus came the Denver sandwich. When a hunter failed to flush a rabbit for supper, she cooked salt pork and corn pone, the Midwest version of New England's johnnycake.

Pheasant Fricassee

½ cup all-purpose flour
2 teaspoons salt
½ teaspoon pepper
2 1½- to 2½-pound ready-to-cook
   pheasants, cut up
6 tablespoons butter or margarine
1 large onion, finely chopped
1 large carrot, finely chopped
1 13¾-ounce can chicken broth
   Dash ground cloves
3 tablespoons all-purpose flour
1 cup light cream
2 tablespoons snipped parsley
1 tablespoon lemon juice

Combine the ½ cup flour, salt, and pepper in paper or plastic bag. Add pheasant, 2 or 3 pieces at a time; shake to coat well. In large heavy skillet brown the pheasant in butter. (Electric skillet 350°.) Add onion and carrot; cook 2 minutes. Add broth and cloves. Reduce heat (200°). Cover and simmer till tender, 45 to 55 minutes. Remove to warm platter. Measure 1 cup broth; return to skillet. In a screw-top jar, shake 3 tablespoons flour and the cream till blended. Stir into broth in skillet; cook and stir till thickened and bubbly. Add parsley and lemon juice. Serve over pheasant. Makes 6 servings.

Denver Sandwich

¼ cup finely chopped onion
2 tablespoons finely chopped
   green pepper
1 tablespoon butter or margarine
4 slightly beaten eggs
½ cup finely chopped fully cooked ham
¼ cup milk
1 tablespoon chopped canned pimiento
8 slices bread, buttered and toasted,
   or 4 buns, split, buttered, and toasted

In skillet cook onion and green pepper in butter till tender. (Electric skillet 300°.) Combine eggs, ham, milk, pimiento, dash salt, and dash pepper. Pour into skillet with onion mixture. Reduce heat (220°). Cook slowly, lifting and folding occasionally, just until set. Spoon mixture between toast slices or onto buns. Serves 4.

Mountain Rainbow Trout

6 large fresh or frozen pan-dressed
   trout
⅔ cup yellow cornmeal
¼ cup all-purpose flour
2 teaspoons salt
½ teaspoon paprika
   Shortening or bacon drippings

Thaw frozen fish; dry with paper toweling. Combine cornmeal, flour, salt, and paprika. Coat fish in mixture. In skillet heat shortening over hot coals till a drop of water sizzles. Brown till fish flakes easily when tested with a fork, about 4 minutes on each side. (Do not overcook.) Makes 6 servings.

Catch a dishpan full for supper

*Good western cooks coat Mountain Rainbow Trout →
with cornmeal, then fry in bacon drippings hot
enough to make the tails curl. Accompanied by plenty
of hot coffee, these delectable fish end the day right.*

Potato Lefse (Norwegian Pancakes)

2 cups hot mashed potatoes
2 tablespoons butter, softened
1 tablespoon milk
1 teaspoon salt
1 cup sifted all-purpose flour
Butter

Beat together hot mashed potatoes, butter, milk, and salt. Cover and chill thoroughly. Turn out on floured surface. Sprinkle with *half* the flour. Knead for 8 to 10 minutes, gradually kneading in remaining flour. Divide dough into 8 or 16 portions; shape into balls.

On floured surface, roll each to a paper-thin circle, small balls to 6-inch, large balls to 9-inch diameter. Roll circle of dough around rolling pin; unroll into hot, lightly greased skillet. (Electric skillet 400°.) Cook till lightly browned on bottom, about 2 or 3 minutes. Turn carefully and brown on other side, about 2 or 3 minutes more. (Lefse should be slightly limp, not crisp.) Repeat with remaining dough. Spread with butter, and sprinkle with sugar, if desired; fold in quarters. Makes 8 large or 16 small lefse.

Note: If desired, lefse may be made ahead, wrapped, and stored in refrigerator or other cool place. To serve, sprinkle each lefse with water, or place it between damp paper toweling. Let stand a few minutes to soften.

Sirloin Especial

4 beef top loin strip steaks, cut
   ¾ inch thick
2 tablespoons butter or margarine
1 3-ounce can sliced mushrooms, drained
¼ cup thinly sliced green onion with tops
1 tablespoon lemon juice
1 clove garlic, minced
¼ teaspoon salt
¼ teaspoon dried basil leaves, crushed

In skillet cook steaks in butter over medium heat to desired doneness, turning once, about 9 minutes for rare, about 11 minutes for medium, or about 20 minutes for well-done. (Electric skillet 350°.) Remove steaks to warm platter. Add mushrooms, onion, lemon juice, garlic, salt, and basil to skillet. Heat till bubbly; serve with steaks. Makes 4 servings.

Pork Chop and Wild Rice Skillet

Pictured on page 42 —

4 loin pork chops, cut ¾ inch thick
½ cup chopped onion
1 cup uncooked wild rice, washed
1 10½-ounce can condensed beef broth
1⅓ cups water
1 medium tomato, sliced

Trim fat from chops and cook trimmings in 10-inch skillet till 2 tablespoons drippings accumulate; remove trimmings. (Electric skillet 350°.) Slowly brown the chops on both sides. Remove chops. Cook onion in pan drippings till tender but not brown. Add rice, broth, and water. Return chops to skillet; season with salt and pepper. Cover; reduce heat to simmer (225°). Cook till chops are tender, 50 to 60 minutes. Place tomato slices on chops; heat through. Serves 4.

Norwegian Fattigmann

This cardamom-spiced cruller, a traditional Scandinavian Christmas sweet, is good with coffee —

2 beaten eggs
¼ cup whipping cream
2 tablespoons sugar
1 tablespoon butter, melted
1 teaspoon lemon juice
1½ cups sifted all-purpose flour
½ teaspoon ground cardamom
¼ teaspoon salt
Cooking oil
Powdered sugar

Mix together eggs, cream, and sugar. Stir in butter and lemon juice. Add flour, cardamom, and salt; mix well. Cover and chill 2 or 3 hours. Divide dough in half; keep 1 portion refrigerated. Roll the other portion ⅛ inch thick on lightly floured surface. Cut into 2-inch diamonds. Cut a slit in the center of each and pull one corner through. Repeat with remaining dough.

In skillet that is at least 3 inches deep, pour in 1½ inches oil; heat to 375°. (Electric skillet, see tip, page 72.) Fry a few at a time till light golden brown, about 2 minutes, turning once. Drain on paper toweling. Sprinkle with powdered sugar while warm. Makes 3½ dozen.

Cinnamon Apples

Use as a meat accompaniment, or serve with vanilla ice cream and some of the cooking syrup for a sundae—

    3 cups sugar
    3 cups water
    ½ cup red cinnamon candies
    6 tart medium apples, cored and cut
        into ½-inch-thick rings
        (2¼ pounds)
    3 tablespoons lemon juice

In 12-inch skillet combine sugar, water, and candies. (Electric skillet 350°.) Heat till candies dissolve. Reduce heat to maintain gentle rolling boil (250°). Brush apple rings with lemon juice to prevent discoloration. Add 8 to 10 apple rings; cook in syrup till tender, turning once, about 2 minutes on each side. Carefully lift apples from syrup with slotted pancake turner. Drain on rack set on baking sheet. Repeat with remaining apples. Serve warm or thoroughly chilled. Use to garnish roast pork, if desired. Makes 30 apple rings.

Fresh Creamed Corn

With a knife, score kernels before cutting corn from the cob; then you'll get all the milk—

    5 ears corn, husked and silked
    2 slices bacon
    ½ cup milk
    ½ teaspoon salt
    ½ teaspoon sugar
    ½ cup light cream
    1½ teaspoons all-purpose flour
    1 tablespoon butter or margarine
        Dash pepper

Cut corn from cob; set aside. In an 8-inch skillet cook bacon till crisp; remove and crumble, reserving drippings. Add corn, milk, salt, and sugar to reserved drippings. Cook, covered, about 15 to 20 minutes, stirring occasionally. In screw-top jar, shake together light cream and flour till combined; stir into corn mixture. Add butter and pepper. Cook, stirring constantly, till thickened and bubbly. Garnish with crumbled bacon. Makes 6 servings.

Split Pea Soup

Hearty whole-meal soups helped early Mormon settlers survive the rigors of settling the mountain West. Like the sheepherders, they ate sourdough bread—

    1½ quarts water
    1 teaspoon salt
    ¼ teaspoon pepper
    ¼ teaspoon dried marjoram leaves,
        crushed
    8 ounces dried green split peas
        (1¼ cups)
    ½ pound bulk pork sausage
    ½ cup chopped celery
    ½ cup peeled, diced potatoes
    ½ cup chopped onion

In large skillet combine water, salt, pepper, and marjoram; bring to boiling. (Electric skillet 250°.) Stir in peas. Cover and simmer 1½ to 2 hours. Shape sausage into 24 balls. Drop into soup; add celery, potatoes, and onion. Cook till vegetables are tender, about 30 minutes more. Makes 4 to 6 servings.

Tomato-Sauced Pork Chops

    4 shoulder pork chops, cut
        ¾ inch thick
    1 medium onion, sliced
    ¼ cup sliced celery
            • • •
    1 10½-ounce can condensed tomato soup
    1 12-ounce can whole kernel corn
    1 cup water
    ½ teaspoon dried thyme leaves, crushed
    ½ teaspoon dried oregano leaves,
        crushed
    ½ medium green pepper, cut in strips

Trim excess fat from chops; cook trimmings in skillet till 1 tablespoon fat accumulates. (Electric skillet 350°.) Discard trimmings and brown the chops on both sides in hot fat. Remove chops; cook onion and celery in same skillet till tender but not brown. Drain off excess fat. Stir in soup, corn, water, thyme, and oregano. Add chops to sauce. Cover and reduce heat (220°). Simmer till tender, 40 to 50 minutes. Add green pepper; cook 5 minutes more. Serve sauce with chops. Makes 4 servings.

SOUTHWEST

Out of the Southwest has come a colorful style of cooking that's a hybrid based on the Mexican tortilla and the Texas barbecue. Barbecuing is the way cowboys cooked meat over an open fire with a highly seasoned sauce of vinegar, vegetables (mostly tomatoes), sugar, and spices (mostly chili powder). It was the only way to deal with a tough critter known as the Texas longhorn. Today, chuck wagon chow calls for a skillet, and barbecuing for pork or beef.

Tortillas are the Mexican woman's favorite convenience food because these thin cornmeal pancakes can be transformed into so many dishes. Fried crisp in hot oil and stacked with ground beef, pork, or chicken for a sandwich, they're tostadas; rolled and filled, they're enchiladas; and stuffed and folded in half, tacos.

Skillet Enchiladas

  1 pound ground beef
  ½ cup chopped onion
  1 10½-ounce can condensed cream of
     mushroom soup
  1 10-ounce can enchilada sauce
  ⅓ cup milk
  2 tablespoons seeded, chopped,
     canned green chilies
  8 frozen, canned, or homemade tortillas
     Cooking oil
2½ cups shredded sharp process American
     cheese (10 ounces)
  ½ cup chopped pitted ripe olives

In a 10-inch skillet brown the ground beef and onion; drain off excess fat. (Electric skillet 350°.) Stir in soup, enchilada sauce, milk, and chilies. Reduce heat (220°); cover and cook 20 minutes, stirring occasionally.

In a small 6-inch skillet dip the tortillas in a little hot cooking oil just till limp. Drain. Reserving ½ cup cheese, place ¼ cup cheese on each tortilla; sprinkle with olives. Roll up each tortilla. Place in sauce; cover and cook till heated through, 5 minutes. Sprinkle with reserved cheese; cover and cook till cheese melts, about 1 minute. Makes 4 servings.

Texas-Style Chili

2¼ pounds beef round steak, cubed
  1 clove garlic, crushed
  3 tablespoons cooking oil
  1 10½-ounce can condensed beef broth
  2 teaspoons sugar
  2 teaspoons dried oregano leaves,
     crushed
  1 to 2 teaspoons cumin seed, crushed
  2 bay leaves
  1 4-ounce jar diced chili peppers,
     seeded and mashed
  2 tablespoons cornmeal

In large skillet brown the steak cubes and garlic in hot oil; drain off excess fat. (Electric skillet 350°.) Add beef broth, 1½ cups water, the sugar, oregano, cumin, ½ teaspoon salt, and bay leaves. Reduce heat (220°.); simmer till meat is tender, about 1½ hours. Stir in chili peppers and cornmeal. Simmer 30 minutes, stirring occasionally. Remove bay leaves. Serve over corn bread, if desired. Makes 4 to 6 servings.

Barbecued Pork Sandwich

COST-CUTTING · RECIPE

  ½ cup chopped onion
  ¼ cup chopped celery
  1 clove garlic, minced
  2 tablespoons butter or margarine
  1 cup chili sauce
  2 tablespoons vinegar
  2 tablespoons brown sugar
  2 tablespoons Worcestershire sauce
  ¾ teaspoon chili powder
  ¼ teaspoon salt
12 thin slices cooked roast pork or beef
  6 hamburger buns, split and toasted

In skillet cook onion, celery, and garlic in butter till tender but not brown. (Electric skillet 350°.) Stir in chili sauce, ½ cup water, the vinegar, brown sugar, Worcestershire, chili powder, salt, and dash pepper. Simmer, covered, 10 to 15 minutes (220°). Add pork; heat through. Serve on buns with sauce. Serves 6.

Skillet Enchiladas are cheese-stuffed tortillas cooked in a ground beef sauce, and seasoned with green chili peppers. Serve them with a tossed salad and a smooth guacamole dressing of mashed avocado.

Skillet Fruit Relish

> 2 cups cubed, peeled pumpkin
>   or winter squash
> 1½ cups chopped, peeled apple
> ½ cup raisins
> ¼ cup shelled sunflower seeds
> 3 tablespoons sugar
> 2 tablespoons vinegar
> ⅛ teaspoon ground cinnamon
> ⅛ teaspoon ground cloves

In medium skillet combine all ingredients with ½ cup water and ¼ teaspoon salt. (Electric skillet 350°.) Bring to boiling. Reduce heat (220°); simmer, covered, till pumpkin is tender, 20 to 30 minutes. Stir carefully to keep pieces whole. Chill. Serve with meats. Makes 3 cups.

Garbanzo Hot Pot

> 1 cup chopped onion
> ¼ cup chopped green pepper
> 2 tablespoons butter
> 2 15-ounce cans garbanzo beans, drained
> 1 13¾-ounce can chicken broth
> 1 cup chopped, peeled tomato
> ¼ teaspoon dried marjoram leaves, crushed
> 1 bay leaf

In large skillet cook onion and green pepper in butter till tender but not brown. (Electric skillet 300°.) Stir in garbanzos, chicken broth, tomato, ½ teaspoon salt, the marjoram, ⅛ teaspoon pepper, and bay leaf. Reduce heat (220°); simmer, uncovered, 20 minutes. Remove bay leaf. Makes 5 servings.

Corn Tortillas

Masa harina is blue if ground from Indian corn; it's sold in supermarkets in the Southwest—

2 cups corn flour (masa harina)
1 cup water

Combine corn flour and water; mix well with hands until dough is moist but will hold its shape. Add more water, if needed. Divide dough into 12 balls. Dampen slightly with water; press between sheets of waxed paper, using a tortilla press or flat baking dish. Carefully peel off top sheet of paper from tortilla.

Place tortilla, paper side up, in hot ungreased skillet. (Electric skillet 350°.) Gently peel off remaining paper. Cook till edges begin to dry, about 30 seconds. Turn and cook till puffs appear in tortilla. Repeat with remaining dough. Spread with butter, fold in quarters, and eat as bread, or fry in hot oil for use in Chili Tostadas or Skillet Enchiladas. Makes 12 tortillas.

For Corn Tortillas, *mix corn flour (extra-fine grind cornmeal called masa harina) with water. Pinch off dough; flatten with a cast-iron press or baking dish.*

Arroz con Pollo (Chicken with Rice)

Saffron is traditional, but to cut cost, omit it—

¼ cup all-purpose flour
1 2- to 2½-pound ready-to-cook
    broiler-fryer chicken, cut up
2 tablespoons cooking oil
½ cup chopped onion
1 clove garlic, minced
2 cups chicken broth
2 tomatoes, chopped (1½ cups)
1 cup uncooked long grain rice
2 tablespoons snipped parsley
1 teaspoon salt
½ teaspoon paprika
¼ teaspoon thread saffron, crushed
⅛ teaspoon pepper
1 bay leaf

Combine flour, ½ teaspoon salt, and ⅛ teaspoon pepper in paper or plastic bag. Add chicken, a few pieces at a time; shake well. In large, heavy skillet brown the chicken slowly in hot oil. (Electric skillet 350°.) Remove chicken. Cook onion and garlic in oil till tender but not brown. Add remaining ingredients. Return chicken to skillet. Cover and cook over low heat till chicken is tender, 40 to 50 minutes. Serves 4.

Chili Tostadas

1 pound ground beef
½ cup chopped onion
1 15-ounce can tomato sauce
1 teaspoon chili powder
½ teaspoon salt
    Few dashes bottled hot pepper sauce
1 15-ounce can pinto beans, undrained
6 to 8 frozen, canned, or homemade
    tortillas, fried
    Shredded cheese
    Shredded lettuce

In large skillet cook ground beef and onion till lightly browned. (Electric skillet 350°.) Drain off excess fat. Add tomato sauce, chili powder, salt, hot pepper sauce, and the *undrained* beans. Reduce heat (220°); simmer, uncovered, for 30 minutes, stirring occasionally. Spoon onto fried tortillas. Top each with some of the cheese and lettuce. Makes 6 to 8 servings.

Chilies Rellenos con Queso
(Green Peppers Stuffed with Cheese)

> 3 fresh, long green hot peppers or canned green chilies
> 1 to 1½ cups shredded sharp natural Cheddar cheese (4 to 6 ounces)
> All-purpose flour
> 6 eggs, separated
> 3 tablespoons all-purpose flour
> Shortening or cooking oil

To prepare fresh peppers, place them on broiler pan 4 inches from heat. Broil just till skins blister. Cool slightly by wrapping in wet towel. Peel and cut peppers in half crosswise; stem and seed. (If using canned chilies, cut in half crosswise.) Stuff peppers with cheese; roll in flour. Beat whites till stiff but not dry. Add 3 tablespoons flour and dash salt to yolks; beat till thick and lemon-colored. Fold into whites.

In skillet that is at least 3 inches deep, heat fat 1 inch deep to 375°. (Electric skillet, see tip, page 72.) For each Chili Relleno, spoon ½ cup of batter into hot fat, spreading into a circle. As batter begins to set, gently top with a pepper. Cover with more batter. Continue cooking till browned, turning once; drain on paper toweling. Serve at once. Makes 6 servings.

Red Rice

> 3 slices bacon
> ½ cup finely chopped onion
> ⅓ cup finely chopped red sweet pepper
> ¾ cup uncooked long grain rice
> 1 16-ounce can tomatoes, cut up
> ¾ teaspoon sugar
> ½ teaspoon paprika
> Dash bottled hot pepper sauce

In medium skillet cook bacon till crisp. (Electric skillet 350°.) Drain, reserving 3 tablespoons drippings, and crumble bacon. Cook onion and red sweet pepper in reserved drippings till tender but not brown. Add rice; cook and stir 2 minutes. Stir in remaining ingredients, 1¼ cups water, and 1 teaspoon salt. Bring to boiling; reduce heat (220°). Cover and simmer till rice is tender and all liquid is absorbed, about 20 minutes. Top with bacon. Makes 12 servings.

Chicken Molé

> 1 2½- to 3-pound ready-to-cook broiler-fryer chicken, cut up
> ¼ cup butter or margarine
> Salt and pepper
> ¼ cup minced onion
> ¼ cup minced green pepper
> 1 small clove garlic, minced
> 1 7½-ounce can tomatoes, cut up
> ½ cup beef broth
> 2 teaspoons sugar
> ½ teaspoon chili powder
> ⅛ teaspoon ground cinnamon
> ⅛ teaspoon ground nutmeg
> Dash ground cloves
> Dash bottled hot pepper sauce
> ¼ of a 1-ounce square unsweetened chocolate
> 1 tablespoon cornstarch

In large, heavy skillet brown the chicken slowly in butter. (Electric skillet 350°.) Season lightly with salt and pepper. Set chicken aside; cover. In same skillet cook onion, green pepper, and garlic in butter remaining in pan. Add remaining ingredients, *except* cornstarch, to skillet. Add chicken. Cover and reduce heat (220°); cook till tender, about 45 minutes. Remove chicken to platter; keep warm. Combine cornstarch with 2 tablespoons cold water; stir into sauce. Cook and stir till thickened and bubbly. Pour sauce over chicken. Makes 4 servings.

Frijoles (Mexican Fried Beans)

> 6 slices bacon
> 2 15-ounce cans kidney beans
> ½ teaspoon salt

In a 10-inch skillet cook bacon till crisp. (Electric skillet 350°.) Drain bacon, reserving 2 tablespoons drippings. Put *1 can* of the *undrained* kidney beans in blender container; add salt, bacon, and the reserved drippings. Adjust lid; blend till beans are mashed. (When necessary, stop blender and use rubber spatula to scrape down sides.) Place mixture in skillet. Drain and add remaining beans, mashing slightly. Cook, uncovered, over low heat, stirring frequently, till thickened, about 10 minutes. Makes 6 servings.

WEST COAST AND HAWAII

Armed with crocks of sourdough for making bread, miners swarmed to California's gold fields in 1849 where they became known as 'sourdoughs.' Some found a richer lode in the mission gardens whose trees and vines provided a more enduring wealth—cuttings for today's orchards and vineyards. The Chinese came to set up restaurants, so soy sauce, kumquats, and gingerroot are no more novelty in cosmopolitan San Francisco than in Hawaii or in the Orient.

Sourdough Starter

> 1 package active dry yeast
> 2½ cups warm water
> 2 cups sifted all-purpose flour
> 1 tablespoon sugar

Dissolve yeast in ½ cup water; stir in remaining water, flour, and sugar. Beat smooth. Cover with cheesecloth; let stand at room temperature for 5 to 10 days, stirring twice a day. If room is warm, let stand the shorter time. Cover; refrigerate till 12 hours before ready to use.

To keep Starter going: Add ¾ cup water, ¾ cup sifted all-purpose flour, and 1 teaspoon sugar to remaining starter after some is used. *Let stand at room temperature till bubbly and well fermented, at least 1 day.* Use or cover and refrigerate. If not used within 10 days, add 1 teaspoon sugar; repeat every 10 days, but no more than 3 times before adding flour.

Golden Delicious Applesauce

> 8 medium Golden Delicious apples,
>   peeled, cored, and diced (3 pounds)
> ½ cup sugar
> ½ teaspoon ground cinnamon
> ⅛ teaspoon ground mace

In skillet combine apples, 1⅔ cups water, the sugar, cinnamon, and mace. (Electric skillet 220°.) Cover and simmer till tender, about 30 minutes. Makes about 4½ cups.

Glazed Duckling

> 1 4½- to 5-pound ready-to-cook frozen
>   duckling, thawed
> 1 teaspoon salt
>   Celery tops
> 1 medium onion, quartered
> ¼ cup honey
> 1 tablespoon soy sauce
> 1 tablespoon all-purpose flour
>   Salt and pepper
>   Preserved kumquats

Pull off fat around tail of duckling. Season duckling with the 1 teaspoon salt; stuff with celery tops and onion. Tie legs and tail together; skewer neck skin to back. Tuck wings under back. Place, breast side up, on rack in electric skillet (325°). Prick with fork to allow fat to escape. Cover and cook 2 hours.

Unplug electric skillet. Cool 5 minutes; remove cover carefully. Pour off fat. Add 1¼ cups water to skillet. Blend honey and soy sauce; baste duckling. Cover and continue cooking at 275° till drumstick moves easily in socket, about 30 minutes longer. Remove duckling to platter, discard onion, celery tops, and string. Baste again with pan juices. Keep hot. Combine flour and ½ cup cold water; stir into skillet. Cook and stir till thickened and bubbly. Season with salt and pepper. Serve with duckling. Garnish with kumquats, if desired. Serve with Braised Celery. Makes 4 servings.

Braised Celery

Remove green outer branches from 2 bunches celery; cut off tops below leaves. Trim root end, but leave attached. Quarter celery lengthwise. Wash well and place in single layer in 10-inch skillet. Dissolve 1 chicken bouillon cube in 1 cup boiling water; add to celery with ¼ cup dry white wine, 2 tablespoons butter or margarine, and dash freshly ground pepper. Cover and simmer till celery is tender, about 25 minutes. Cut crosswise into serving-sized pieces. Spoon sauce over celery. Makes 4 servings.

Glazed Duckling emerges moist, tender, and beautifully browned after 2½ hours in your electric skillet and a basting of soy sauce, honey, and pan drippings. Serve it with Braised Celery and preserved kumquats.

Sourdough Pancakes

    1 cup sifted all-purpose flour
    2 tablespoons sugar
1½ teaspoons baking powder
    ½ teaspoon salt
    ½ teaspoon baking soda
    1 beaten egg
    1 cup Sourdough Starter,
       room temperature
    ½ cup milk
    2 tablespoons cooking oil

Sift together first 5 ingredients. Combine remaining ingredients; stir into flour mixture. Using 2 tablespoons batter for each pancake, bake in hot, lightly greased electric skillet (350°) till golden, turning once. Makes 28 pancakes.

Hangtown Fry

In California gold rush days, when a miner demanded the most expensive meal in Hangtown, the cook scrambled eggs with oysters —

Beat together 6 eggs, ⅓ cup milk, and ½ teaspoon salt. Mix together ¼ cup all-purpose flour, ½ teaspoon salt, and dash pepper. Roll 12 medium-sized shucked oysters in the seasoned flour mixture till thoroughly coated.

    Melt 2 tablespoons butter or margarine in skillet. (Electric skillet 350°.) Cook oysters in butter till edges curl, about 1 minute on each side. Pour egg mixture into skillet. As eggs begin to set on bottom and sides, lift and fold over with wide spatula. Cook till eggs are set throughout, 4 to 5 minutes. Serves 3 or 4.

Chinese Beef and Broccoli

      1 pound beef sirloin steak, cut ½ inch
          thick
      4 teaspoons cornstarch
      2 tablespoons soy sauce
      2 teaspoons cooking oil
      1 teaspoon salt
      1 pound fresh broccoli or 2 10-ounce
          packages frozen broccoli spears
      1 thin slice fresh gingerroot or
          ½ teaspoon ground ginger
      3 tablespoons cooking oil
      2 green onions with tops, thinly
          sliced (2 tablespoons)
              • • •
          Hot cooked rice

Partially freeze beef; slice diagonally in 3x¼-inch strips. Combine cornstarch, soy sauce, the 2 teaspoons oil, and salt in bowl. Add beef; toss to coat well. Slice broccoli lengthwise in thin strips, 3 inches long.

Heat ginger in 3 tablespoons oil in electric wok or skillet at 375°. Add broccoli and stir-fry 3 to 5 minutes. Remove from pan. (Cook *half* the broccoli or beef at a time when using a wok.) Add more oil, if necessary, and stir-fry beef till well browned, 5 minutes. Return broccoli to pan; add ½ cup water. Cook and stir till gravy is thickened and clear. Garnish with green onion slices. Serve with hot cooked rice. Makes 4 servings.

Roll thin pancakes made with cornstarch around a delicious shrimp filling for Egg Rolls. *Fry at once in hot oil, or refrigerate to fry later.*

Egg Rolls

      ½ cup bean sprouts, drained
      ½ cup finely chopped, cooked pork
      ¼ cup finely chopped, cooked shrimp
      ¼ cup finely chopped celery
      ¼ cup water chestnuts, rinsed, drained,
          and finely chopped
      1 tablespoon finely chopped onion
      1 slightly beaten egg
      1 tablespoon cooking oil
      1 teaspoon soy sauce
      ½ teaspoon sugar
      ¼ teaspoon salt
          Chinese Pancakes
          Cooking oil

Combine the first 11 ingredients; chill. Prepare *Chinese Pancakes:* In mixing bowl sift together 1⅓ cups sifted all-purpose flour, ⅔ cup cornstarch, and 1 teaspoon salt. Combine 2 beaten eggs and 1½ cups water. Gradually blend eggs into flour mixture. Beat till smooth. Lightly grease a 6-inch heavy skillet; heat. Reserve ½ cup batter for sealing edges. Add 2 tablespoons remaining batter to pan; tilt to spread evenly over bottom. Cook over medium heat till top looks dry and edges begin to curl. Do not turn. Place on paper towels. Repeat with remaining batter, greasing pan occasionally.

To assemble egg rolls, place 1 tablespoon filling near edge of pancake. Brush edges with reserved batter. Fold edge over filling; fold in both sides. Roll up, pressing gently to seal. In skillet that is at least 3 inches deep, heat 1½ inches oil to 375°. (Electric skillet, see tip, page 72.) Fry, a few at a time, about 6 minutes. Drain on paper toweling. Repeat till all are cooked. Serve with bottled hot mustard and sweet-sour sauces, if desired. Makes 18.

Pineapple-Glazed Bananas

Cut up 2 cups fresh pineapple over bowl, catching juice. Add water to juice, if necessary, to make ½ cup. In skillet combine pineapple with juice, ⅓ cup brown sugar, 2 tablespoons honey, and 1 tablespoon butter. (Electric skillet 350°.) Cook and stir 2 minutes. Reduce heat. Peel and halve 5 bananas lengthwise. Add to skillet; simmer till heated through and glazed, turning once. Makes 4 to 6 servings.

Chicken-Papaya Dish

    2 tablespoons all-purpose flour
    1 teaspoon curry powder
    ½ teaspoon salt
    ⅛ teaspoon pepper
    4 small whole, or 2 large, halved
        chicken breasts
    2 tablespoons shortening
    ½ cup chopped onion
    2 teaspoons curry powder
    1 cup light cream
    1 chicken bouillon cube
    1 small papaya

Combine flour, 1 teaspoon curry powder, salt, and the pepper in paper or plastic bag. Add chicken; shake to coat. In medium skillet brown the chicken in hot shortening. (Electric skillet 350°.) Remove chicken to platter and keep warm, reserving drippings.

Cook onion in drippings till tender but not brown. Stir in 2 teaspoons curry powder, the light cream, and bouillon cube. Return chicken to skillet; cover and cook over low heat till done, 40 minutes. Peel and slice papaya into 8 wedges; discard seeds. Add papaya to skillet; cover and heat through. Makes 4 servings.

Grilled Abalone

This Pacific coast conch clings so tightly to underwater rocks that it takes a tire iron to pry it loose—

    1 pound fresh or frozen abalone steaks
    ⅓ cup all-purpose flour
    1 teaspoon salt
    ¼ teaspoon pepper
    1 beaten egg
    1 tablespoon milk
    1½ cups fine saltine cracker crumbs
    ¼ cup butter or margarine
        Lemon wedges

Thaw frozen abalone steaks. Combine flour, salt, and pepper. Combine egg and milk. Dip steaks in seasoned flour, then in egg mixture. Coat with cracker crumbs. Melt butter in skillet. (Electric skillet 350°.) Cook steaks 1 minute on each side. *Do not overcook, or they will be tough.* Drain on paper toweling. Serve piping hot with lemon wedges. Makes 4 servings.

Poached Salmon

    4 fresh or frozen salmon steaks, cut
        1 inch thick (1 pound)
    1¼ cups dry white wine
    2 tablespoons thinly sliced green
        onion with tops
    2 or 3 sprigs parsley
    1 bay leaf
    1 teaspoon salt
        Dash pepper
    ¼ cup whipping cream
    2 well-beaten egg yolks
    ½ teaspoon lemon juice
    2 tablespoons snipped parsley

Thaw frozen salmon. In skillet combine wine, onion, parsley sprigs, bay leaf, salt, and pepper. (Electric skillet 350°.) Heat to boiling; add salmon steaks. Cover and reduce heat (220°); simmer till fish flakes easily when tested with fork, about 10 minutes. Remove fish and bay leaf. Keep salmon steaks warm.

Boil wine mixture down to ¾ cup. Combine cream, egg yolks, and lemon juice; slowly add *part* of wine mixture. Return to wine mixture in skillet. Cook and stir over low heat till thickened and bubbly. Spoon over fish. Garnish with snipped parsley. Makes 4 servings.

Lamb Chops à la Grecque

California consumes more lamb than any other state, partly because of its large population of Armenian and Greek descent around Fresno—

    3 tablespoons olive oil
    1 tablespoon lemon juice
    ¾ teaspoon salt
    ½ teaspoon dried oregano leaves, crushed
    ¼ teaspoon freshly ground pepper
    4 shoulder lamb chops, cut 1 inch thick
        (about 1 pound)

COST-CUTTING RECIPE

Combine oil, lemon juice, salt, oregano, and pepper in plastic bag. Add lamb chops; marinate 2 to 4 hours in refrigerator. Drain, reserving marinade. Using marinade, brown the meat on both sides in heavy 10-inch skillet over medium-low heat till done—10 minutes for medium-rare; 15 minutes for well-done. (Electric skillet 275°.) Makes 4 servings.

Skillet Specialties

Give your skillets some extra jobs to do. Use them often as a vegetable cooker, a sauce pot, a griddle, a shallow-fat fryer, a steamer, or an oven. (The controlled heat of the electric frypan is especially helpful when temperature is important to success.)

A skillet is just right for cooking odd-sized vegetables such as corn on the cob or asparagus. It's also handy for making smooth gravies.

Use your largest skillet as a griddle for pancakes or English muffins. Learn how to use a heavy, deep skillet for frying doughnuts and other sweets. Choose this heavy pan for candymaking tasks, too.

Turn out a tempting array of fast or fancy desserts from your skillets. Simmer or poach some, but bake or steam the others in these versatile pans.

Skillet-poached meringues topped with caramelized sugar and set adrift on smooth custard are the ingredients in elegant *Caramel Floating Island.* Complete directions are on page 77.

California Artichokes

4 medium artichokes
Water
2 tablespoons vinegar
2 tablespoons cooking oil
1 teaspoon salt
4 or 5 peppercorns
1 bay leaf
Mayonnaise or salad dressing

With sharp knife cut stems, discolored leaves, and 1 inch from tops of artichokes; trim off sharp leaf tips with kitchen shears. Place artichokes in a large skillet that is at least 3 inches deep. Add water to depth of ½ inch, the vinegar, oil, salt, peppercorns, and bay leaf. (Electric skillet 250°.) Cover; simmer till stem is tender and leaf pulls easily from base, 20 to 25 minutes. Drain; turn upside down on board, and press gently to remove water. Serve hot or cold with mayonnaise. Pull off petals one by one and dip pulpy end in mayonnaise; draw between teeth, and discard remainder of petal. Makes 4 servings.

Ratatouille (All-Vegetable Stew)

Thyme, tomatoes, and garlic mark this recipe as a favorite of southern France—

1¾ cups coarsely chopped onion
1 clove garlic, minced
2 tablespoons cooking oil
½ pound eggplant, cut in ½-inch strips
½ pound zucchini, cut in strips
2 green peppers, cut in strips
4 medium tomatoes, coarsely chopped
1 teaspoon salt
Dash freshly ground pepper
2 or 3 fresh basil leaves, snipped, or 1 teaspoon dried basil leaves, crushed
2 sprigs fresh thyme, snipped, or ½ teaspoon dried thyme leaves, crushed

In large skillet cook onion and garlic in oil till tender but not brown. (Electric skillet 300°.) Add remaining ingredients. Cover; bring to boiling. Reduce heat (220°). Simmer 40 minutes, stirring occasionally. Take care not to break up vegetable pieces. Serve hot as a vegetable side dish or cold as an hors d' oeuvre. Serves 6 to 8.

Squash and Apples

3 small acorn squash
Salt
2 large apples, peeled, cored, and chopped
⅓ cup brown sugar
¼ cup raisins
2 tablespoons butter or margarine

Cut squash in half lengthwise; remove seeds and stringy portions. Place in electric skillet (350°), cut side down; add 1 cup water. Cover and bring to boiling. Reduce heat (220°); simmer 20 to 25 minutes with vent open. Turn squash cut side up; sprinkle with salt. Combine apples, brown sugar, and raisins; spoon into squash. Dot with butter. Cover; cook till tender, about 15 to 20 minutes. Makes 6 servings.

Sweet and Sour Asparagus Salad

1 pound fresh asparagus spears
6 slices bacon
¼ cup wine vinegar
4 teaspoons sugar
⅛ teaspoon salt
Dash pepper
2 green onions, finely chopped
6 cups torn lettuce, well drained
2 hard-cooked eggs, sliced

In skillet spread out asparagus; cook in small amount of boiling, salted water till tender, 8 minutes. (Electric skillet 275°.) Drain asparagus and set aside. In skillet cook bacon till crisp. Drain, reserving 2 tablespoons drippings; crumble bacon. To reserved drippings in skillet add vinegar, ¼ cup water, sugar, salt, pepper, onions, and asparagus; heat through. Remove asparagus; toss lettuce with hot dressing 1 minute. Arrange on plates with asparagus, egg slices, and bacon. Serves 6.

Lend variety to meals

One advantage of cooking vegetables in a skillet is → that they can be left in big pieces, as were the tender spears for this Sweet and Sour Asparagus Salad. *The hot dressing comes from the Pennsylvania Dutch.*

Herb-Topped Butter Beans

   2 tablespoons butter or margarine
   ¼ cup fine dry bread crumbs
   ⅛ teaspoon dried sage leaves, crushed
   ⅛ teaspoon dried marjoram leaves,
      crushed
   1 tablespoon all-purpose flour
   1 teaspoon dried mustard
   1 cup milk
   ½ cup process cheese spread or cold-
      pack cheese food
   2 16-ounce cans butter beans, drained

In skillet melt 1 *tablespoon* of the butter; add crumbs and brown lightly. Stir in herbs; set aside. Melt remaining butter; blend in flour and mustard; stir in milk. Cook, stirring constantly, till thick and smooth. Add cheese and continue cooking and stirring till cheese melts. Add butter beans; blend with cheese sauce. Heat through. Top with crumbs. Serves 6.

Mexican Rarebit

   2 tablespoons chopped green pepper
   2 tablespoons butter or margarine
   1 7½-ounce can tomatoes
   2 cups shredded sharp process American
      cheese (8 ounces)
   1 20-ounce can whole kernel corn,
      drained
   1 well-beaten egg
   ½ cup soft bread crumbs
   ¼ teaspoon chili powder
      Toast points

In skillet cook green pepper in butter till tender. (Electric skillet 300°.) Add tomatoes and cheese; stir till cheese melts. Combine corn and egg; add to tomato mixture. Add crumbs, chili powder, and dash salt. Heat through, stirring constantly. Serve piping hot cheese mixture on toast points. Makes 6 servings.

Corn on the Cob

Husk corn; remove silk with stiff brush. Cook, covered, in small amount boiling, salted water in large skillet 6 to 8 minutes. (Electric skillet 275°.) Serve with salt and butter.

Skillet-Style French Fries

   3 medium baking potatoes (1½ pounds)
      Cooking oil
      Salt

Peel potatoes and cut lengthwise in ⅜- or ½-inch-wide strips. In skillet that is at least 3 inches deep, heat 1 inch of oil to 360°. (Electric skillet, see tip, page 72.) Fry a few potatoes at a time till crisp and golden, 6 or 7 minutes. Drain on paper toweling. Sprinkle with salt. Serve at once. Makes 4 servings.
   For crisper French fries: Cook at 360° till lightly browned, about 5 minutes. Drain on paper toweling and cool. Just before serving, return French fries to oil at 360° for 2 minutes more. Drain, season, and serve at once.

French-Fried Onion Rings

   1 large onion, cut in ¼-inch slices
   1 cup packaged pancake mix
   ¼ teaspoon salt
      Cooking oil

Separate onion into rings. Combine pancake mix, salt, and ⅔ cup cold water in bowl. Beat about 2 minutes. Dip onion rings in batter; drain. In skillet that is at least 3 inches deep, heat 1½ inches of oil to 375°. (Electric skillet, see tip, page 72.) Fry onion rings till brown, 2 or 3 minutes. Drain thoroughly on paper toweling. Makes 6 garnish or 3 vegetable servings.

Cheese-Frosted Cauliflower

   1 medium head cauliflower
   ½ cup mayonnaise
   2 teaspoons prepared mustard
   ¾ cup shredded sharp process American
      cheese (3 ounces)

Remove leaves and trim base from cauliflower. Wash. Precook in boiling, salted water 12 to 15 minutes. (Electric skillet 275°.) Drain. Place in pie plate on low rack in skillet. Sprinkle with salt. Combine mayonnaise and mustard; spread over cauliflower. Top with cheese. Cover and cook at 375° till cheese is bubbly, about 5 minutes. Makes 4 to 5 servings.

White Sauce (Medium)

> 2 tablespoons butter or margarine
> 2 tablespoons all-purpose flour
> ¼ teaspoon salt
>   Dash white pepper
> 1 cup milk

In small skillet melt butter over low heat. Blend in flour, salt, and pepper. Add milk all at once. Cook, stirring constantly, till mixture thickens, about 5 minutes. Makes 1 cup.

Thin White Sauce: Use only 1 tablespoon butter and 1 tablespoon all-purpose flour.

Thick White Sauce: Use 3 tablespoons butter and 4 tablespoons all-purpose flour.

Allemande Sauce

> 2 tablespoons butter or margarine
> 2 tablespoons all-purpose flour
> 1 cup chicken broth
> ¼ teaspoon salt
>   Dash white pepper
> ⅓ cup light cream
> 1 beaten egg yolk
> 1 tablespoon lemon juice
>   Dash ground nutmeg

Melt butter in a small skillet over low heat; blend in flour. Add broth, salt, and dash pepper. Cook and stir till thickened. Add cream. Gradually stir ½ *cup* of hot mixture into egg yolk; return to hot mixture. Cook and stir over low heat till thickened; remove from heat. Add lemon juice and nutmeg. Makes 1⅓ cups.

Onion Gravy

Remove cooked beef to hot platter. Skim fat from pan juices, reserving 2 tablespoons fat. Measure juices; add water to make 2 cups. Brown ¼ cup sugar in reserved fat. (Electric skillet 300°.) Add 2 medium onions, thinly sliced. Reduce heat; cook till tender. Push onions to one side. Add 2 tablespoons all-purpose flour; brown the flour slightly. Stir in meat juices, 1 tablespoon vinegar, and ¼ teaspoon Kitchen Bouquet. Cook and stir till thickened and bubbly; boil 2 to 3 minutes. Season with salt and pepper. Makes 6 servings.

Use a whisk to make Perfect Skillet Gravy; *the wire loops smooth out lumps better than a spoon. A heavy skillet and low heat prevent scorching.*

Perfect Skillet Gravy

Remove cooked meat to hot serving platter; keep warm. Leaving crusty bits in skillet, pour juices and fat into large measuring cup. Skim off fat, reserving 3 to 4 tablespoons fat.

For 2 cups gravy, return reserved fat to skillet. Stir in ¼ cup all-purpose flour. Cook and stir over low heat till bubbly and smooth. (Electric skillet 250°.)

Remove skillet from heat or turn temperature control of electric skillet to 'off.' Add 2 cups liquid (meat juices plus water, milk, or broth) all at once; blend till smooth with wire whisk. Season with salt and pepper. If desired, add a dash crushed dried thyme leaves and a few drops Kitchen Bouquet. Simmer, stirring constantly, for 2 to 3 minutes. (Electric skillet 250°.) Makes 6 to 8 servings.

Hurry-Up Cream Gravy

Remove cooked meat from skillet to hot serving platter. Skim off excess fat from juices. Pour ¼ cup water into pan. Stir well to loosen crusty bits on bottom of pan. Blend in one 10½-ounce can condensed cream of chicken *or* cream of mushroom soup. Heat and stir over low heat. (Electric skillet 250°.) Thin with more water, if necessary. Makes about 1½ cups.

Serve a stack of Apple-Raisin Pancakes with butter and a pitcher of maple-flavored syrup. Accompany this breakfast treat with brown-and-serve sausages.

Israeli Cheese Blintzes

    ¾ cup sifted all-purpose flour or
        ½ cup matzo meal
    1 cup milk
    2 beaten eggs
    1½ cups well-drained cream-style
        cottage cheese
    1 beaten egg
    2 tablespoons sugar
    ½ teaspoon vanilla
        Dash ground cinnamon
        Shortening
        Dairy sour cream
        Cherry preserves

Mix flour or matzo meal and ½ teaspoon salt. Combine milk and 2 eggs; gradually add to flour, beating till smooth. Pour about 2 tablespoons batter into hot, lightly greased 6-inch skillet; quickly swirl pan to spread batter evenly. Cook over medium heat till golden on bottom, about 2 minutes. Loosen; turn out of skillet. Repeat with remaining batter.

   Blend together the cottage cheese, 1 egg, sugar, vanilla, and cinnamon. Place pancakes cooked side up; spoon some filling in center of each. Overlap sides atop filling, then overlap ends. Brown on both sides in small amount of hot shortening. Serve hot. Top with sour cream and preserves. Serves 6 or 7.

Apple-Raisin Pancakes

    1 14-ounce package apple-cinnamon
        muffin mix
    2 eggs
    ⅔ cup water
    2 tablespoons cooking oil
    ½ cup raisins

In bowl combine the apple-cinnamon muffin mix, eggs, and water. Beat till mixture is smooth. Stir in the cooking oil and raisins. Using 2 tablespoons of the batter for each, cook pancakes over high heat in a lightly oiled skillet. (Electric skillet 350°.) Watch pancakes carefully so that they do not burn. Makes two dozen 2½-inch or one dozen 5-inch pancakes.

Butterscotch Dessert Pancakes

    1 cup pancake mix
    1 3¾-ounce package regular
        butterscotch pudding mix
    1 cup milk
    2 eggs
    2 tablespoons cooking oil
    ½ cup dairy sour cream
    2 10-ounce packages frozen
        strawberries, thawed

In bowl combine first 5 ingredients; beat with rotary beater just till combined. Drop 1 tablespoon of batter for each pancake into hot, lightly greased skillet, making 30 pancakes. Bake till golden, turning once. (Electric skillet 350°.) Keep warm. For each serving, arrange 5 pancakes on plate; top with a dollop of sour cream and some berries. Serves 6.

English Muffins

 1 package active dry yeast
 5¾ to 6 cups sifted all-purpose flour
 2 cups milk
 ¼ cup shortening
 2 tablespoons sugar
 2 teaspoons salt

In large mixer bowl combine yeast and *2¼ cups* flour. Heat milk, shortening, sugar, and salt just till warm, stirring occasionally to melt shortening. Add to dry mixture in mixing bowl. Beat at low speed with electric mixer for ½ minute, scraping sides of bowl constantly. Beat 3 minutes at high speed. By hand, stir in enough of the remaining flour to make a moderately stiff dough. Turn out on lightly floured surface; knead till smooth, 8 to 10 minutes. Place in greased bowl, turning once. Cover; let rise till double, 1¼ hours. Punch down dough; cover and let rest 10 minutes. Roll dough to slightly less than ½-inch thickness on lightly floured surface. Cut with a 3-inch round cutter. (Reroll edges.) Cover; let rise in warm place till very light, 1¼ hours. Bake on top of range in medium-hot greased skillet. (Electric skillet 325°.) Turn muffins frequently till done, about 30 minutes. Cool thoroughly. Split muffins with a fork; toast both sides. Spread with butter or margarine. Serve at once. Makes 24 muffins.

Skillet-Toasted Muffins

Split English muffins. Spread muffin halves generously with butter or margarine. Place muffins, buttered side down, in skillet. Heat over low heat till muffins are toasty and lightly browned. (Electric skillet 250°.)

Cheese Biscuits

In an electric skillet set at 250° to 260°, melt 2 to 3 tablespoons butter or margarine. Place 1 package refrigerated biscuits (10 biscuits) in skillet so they do not touch. Bake, covered, with vent open for 5 minutes. Turn biscuits and bake 5 minutes more. Top each biscuit with a spoonful of process cheese spread or crumbled blue cheese. Continue baking till cheese melts, about ½ minute. Makes 10.

Skillet Scones

 1 cup sifted all-purpose flour
 3 tablespoons sugar
 2 teaspoons baking powder
 ½ teaspoon salt
 6 tablespoons butter or margarine
 1 cup quick-cooking rolled oats
 ½ cup currants
 2 beaten eggs
 Cooking oil

In mixing bowl sift together flour, sugar, baking powder, and salt. Using pastry blender, cut in butter till crumbly. Stir in oats and currants. Stir in beaten eggs till moistened.

 On waxed paper pat dough to a 8x7-inch rectangle, ½ inch thick. Cut into 12 rectangles, each about 2½x2 inches. Brush 12-inch skillet lightly with oil. In skillet bake scones, covered, over medium-low heat till golden brown on bottom, about 10 minutes. (Electric skillet 275°.) Turn and brown other side in covered skillet 5 minutes more. Serve warm. Makes 12.

Fruited Brown Bread

 1 cup sifted all-purpose flour
 1 teaspoon baking powder
 1 teaspoon baking soda
 1 teaspoon salt
 1 cup yellow cornmeal
 1 cup stirred whole wheat flour
 • • •
 2 cups buttermilk
 ¾ cup dark molasses
 1 cup raisins
 ½ cup mixed candied fruits and peels

Thoroughly grease four 16-ounce fruit or vegetable cans. Sift together flour, baking powder, soda, and salt; stir in cornmeal and whole wheat flour. Add buttermilk, molasses, raisins, and candied fruits; beat well. Divide batter equally among the 4 cans. Cover tops of cans tightly with foil. Place in electric skillet with dome lid.

 Add water to skillet to 1-inch depth. Cover skillet, close vent, and set temperature at simmer (250°). Steam till done, about 2¼ hours, adding more hot water as needed. Remove bread from cans. Cool on rack. Wrap and store overnight. Makes 4 round loaves.

To shallow-fat fry in a skillet

• Use a skillet at least 3 inches deep to allow for 1½ inches cooking oil. This means you'll need about 3 quarts in a 12-inch electric skillet.

• Set heat control of electric skillet at 400° to 450° to maintain a fat temperature of 360° to 375°. Check with deep-fat thermometer or a 1-inch cube of bread. If bread browns in 1 minute, fat is hot enough to fry most foods.

• Add a few pieces of food at a time so fat doesn't cool down too much. Food fried at a low temperature is greasy.

• Use cottonseed or corn oil, or hydrogenated vegetable fats. They can be heated to higher temperature without smoking than lard, bacon fat, or butter.

• Take good care of fat after frying, and you will be able to use it again. Allow the fat to cool, then strain it to remove crumbs. Refrigerate it in a covered jar. When reusing the fat, add some fresh oil or shortening to it.

Coconut Cake Doughnuts

    2 eggs
 ½ cup sugar
 ¼ cup milk
    2 tablespoons shortening, melted
 2⅓ cups sifted all-purpose flour
    2 teaspoons baking powder
 ½ teaspoon salt
 ¾ cup flaked coconut
    Cooking oil

Beat eggs with sugar till light; add milk and cooled shortening. Sift together flour, baking powder, and salt; add with coconut to eggs, stirring just till blended. Cover and chill several hours. Roll ½ inch thick on lightly floured surface. Cut with 2½-inch doughnut cutter.

In a skillet that is at least 3 inches deep, heat 1½ inches oil to 375°. (Electric skillet, see tip, this page.) Fry in oil till brown, 1 minute per side. Drain on paper toweling. Warm doughnuts may be sugared, if desired. Makes 1 dozen.

Country-Style Doughnut Puffs

    2 beaten eggs
 ½ teaspoon vanilla
 ½ cup sugar
 ½ cup light cream
    2 cups sifted all-purpose flour
 1½ teaspoons baking powder
 ½ teaspoon salt
    2 tablespoons butter, melted
    Cooking oil
    1 cup sifted powdered sugar
 ¼ teaspoon ground nutmeg

Beat eggs, vanilla, and sugar well. Stir in cream. Sift together dry ingredients; gradually stir into egg mixture. Fold in melted butter. In skillet that is at least 3 inches deep, heat 1½ inches oil to 375°. (Electric skillet, see tip, this page.) Drop dough by teaspoonfuls into hot oil. Balls should be no more than ¾ inch in diameter to cook through. Fry till brown, turning once, 2 or 3 minutes. Drain on paper toweling; cool. Combine powdered sugar and nutmeg in paper or plastic bag. Shake a few puffs at a time to coat well. Makes 3 to 3½ dozen.

Bunuelos (Colombian Crisps)

 ¾ cup milk
 ¼ cup butter or margarine
    1 tablespoon aniseed, lightly crushed
    2 beaten eggs
    3 cups sifted all-purpose flour
    1 teaspoon baking powder
    1 teaspoon salt
    Cooking oil
 ½ cup sugar
    1 teaspoon ground cinnamon

In saucepan heat milk, butter, and aniseed to boiling; cool. Stir in beaten eggs. Sift together dry ingredients; add egg mixture and mix well. Knead dough on lightly floured surface till smooth, 2 or 3 minutes. Shape into 20 balls. Let rest 5 minutes. Roll each ball into a 4-inch circle. In skillet at least 3 inches deep, heat 1½ inches oil to 375°. (Electric skillet, see tip, this page.) Fry till brown, about 4 minutes, turning once. Drain on paper toweling. Combine sugar and cinnamon in paper or plastic bag; shake crisps, a few at a time. Makes 20.

Apple Fritters

  1 cup sifted all-purpose flour
  2 tablespoons sugar
  2 teaspoons baking powder
  ¼ teaspoon salt
  1 beaten egg
  ⅔ cup milk
  2 tablespoons butter, melted
  3 or 4 apples, peeled and cored, or 18
     thin pineapple slices
     Cooking oil

Sift together dry ingredients. Combine egg, milk, and butter. Stir into dry ingredients till smooth; do not overbeat. Slice apples crosswise into rings; dip in batter one at a time. (Add more milk or flour, if necessary, so batter coats fruit.) In skillet at least 3 inches deep, heat 1½ inches oil to 375°. (Electric skillet, see tip, page 72.) Fry fritters till brown, about 3 minutes, turning once. Drain on paper toweling. Serve hot. Sprinkle with powdered sugar, if desired. Makes 18.

Les Oreillettes (Little Ears)

  2 cups sifted all-purpose flour
  2 tablespoons sugar
  1 tablespoon baking powder
  ½ teaspoon salt
  ¼ teaspoon ground nutmeg
  ⅓ cup milk
  2 eggs
  1 tablespoon grated lemon peel
  1 tablespoon lemon juice
     Cooking oil
     Sifted powdered sugar

Sift together first 5 ingredients; make well in center. Add the milk, eggs, lemon peel, and juice. Mix till well combined. Cover and chill thoroughly, 2 hours or more. Roll out half the dough at a time on lightly floured surface to ⅛-inch thickness. Cut into 2½-inch rounds. Roll each to a 5-inch oblong. Let dry on towel while rolling remaining dough.

In skillet that is at least 3 inches deep, heat 1 inch oil to 375°. (Electric skillet, see tip, page 72.) Fry 5 or 6 cookies at a time till puffed and light golden, 1 to 2 minutes per side. Drain on paper toweling; sprinkle with sifted powdered sugar while warm. Makes 36.

Empanaditas (Little Turnovers)

  2 cups sifted all-purpose flour
  2 teaspoons baking powder
  1 teaspoon salt
  ½ cup shortening
  ½ to ⅔ cup ice water
  ¾ cup chopped blanched almonds
  ½ cup sugar
  1 teaspoon ground cinnamon
  1 egg white
  ¼ teaspoon almond extract
     Cooking oil

Sift together first 3 ingredients. Cut in shortening till mixture resembles coarse crumbs. Add ice water, *1 tablespoon* at a time, tossing with fork till all flour is moistened. Shape into ball. On lightly floured surface, roll ⅛ inch thick. Cut into 2½-inch circles.

Mix almonds, sugar, and cinnamon. Beat egg white with almond extract till frothy; stir in almond mixture. Place 1 teaspoon filling on half of each circle. Wet edges; fold unfilled half over and seal with tines of fork. In skillet at least 3 inches deep, heat 1½ inches oil to 375°. (Electric skillet, see tip, page 72.) Fry till golden brown, about 4 minutes, turning once. Drain on paper toweling. Makes 3 dozen.

Fried Pies

  1 package piecrust mix for 2-crust pie
  1 21-ounce can apple pie filling
  1 teaspoon ground cinnamon
  ½ cup shredded natural Cheddar cheese
     Cooking oil
     Sifted powdered sugar

Prepare piecrust mix according to package directions. On lightly floured surface roll dough ⅛ inch thick; cut into 6-inch circles, using saucer for pattern. Reroll remaining dough; cut into 6-inch circles. Combine pie filling and cinnamon; place ¼ cup on half of each circle. Top with 1 tablespoon cheese. Fold unfilled half over and seal edges with fingers or fork.

In heavy skillet heat ¼ inch oil to 375°. (Electric skillet, see tip, page 72.) Fry pies till brown, about 3 to 4 minutes on each side. Remove carefully to paper toweling; sprinkle with powdered sugar. Makes 7 or 8.

Rabanados (Fried Sweet Bread)

    Cooking oil
 1 3-ounce package ladyfingers, split
 2 well-beaten eggs
 ½ cup sugar
 ½ cup water
    Dash ground cinnamon
 1 tablespoon Port
    Pine nuts

In skillet that is at least 3 inches deep, heat 1½ inches oil to 375°. (Electric skillet, see tip, page 72.) Dip ladyfinger halves into beaten egg, coating completely. Fry in hot oil, turning once, 2 minutes per side. Drain on paper toweling. Keep ladyfingers warm in oven.

Combine sugar, water, and cinnamon in a saucepan. Bring to boiling; boil till slightly thickened, about 10 minutes. Stir in wine. Simmer 3 to 4 minutes more. Pour some of the syrup over ladyfingers. Sprinkle with additional cinnamon and pine nuts. Pass remaining syrup. Makes 8 to 10 servings.

Sonhos (Dreams)

 ½ cup water
 ¼ cup butter or margarine
 2 teaspoons sugar
    Dash salt
 ½ cup sifted all-purpose flour
 2 eggs
    Cooking oil
 ½ cup sugar
 1 teaspoon ground cinnamon

In saucepan combine water, butter, the 2 teaspoons sugar, and the salt. Bring to boiling, stirring till butter melts. Add flour all at once. Cook and stir over low heat till mixture forms a ball that does not separate.

Remove from heat and vigorously beat in eggs, one at a time, till mixture is smooth and shiny. In skillet that is at least 3 inches deep, heat 1½ inches oil to 375°. (Electric skillet, see tip, page 72.) Drop by rounded teaspoonfuls into hot fat; fry, turning once, till golden brown, about 4 minutes. Remove with slotted spoon and drain on paper toweling. Combine the ½ cup sugar and the cinnamon in paper or plastic bag. Shake puffs in sugar mixture. Makes about 30.

Nogados (Portuguese Christmas Log)

Tiny 'twigs' of fried dough—240 of them stuck together with honey syrup—form this yule log that is similar to a Sicilian dessert made in a tree shape—

 1¼ cups sifted all-purpose flour
 1   tablespoon sugar
 ¼   teaspoon salt
 2   tablespoons shortening
 2   beaten eggs
 ½   teaspoon grated lemon peel
     Cooking oil
 ½   cup sugar
 ½   cup honey
 ½   teaspoon vanilla
 ¼   teaspoon ground cinnamon

In large bowl sift together flour, the 1 tablespoon sugar, and the salt. Cut in shortening till mixture resembles coarse crumbs. Add beaten eggs and grated lemon peel; mix well. Turn dough out onto lightly floured surface. Roll dough to 15x12-inch rectangle, ⅛ inch thick. Cut crosswise into five 3-inch pieces; cut each piece into strips ¼ inch wide and 3 inches long.

In skillet at least 3 inches deep, heat 1½ inches cooking oil to 375°. (Electric skillet, see tip, page 72.) Fry a few at a time about 4 minutes, turning once or twice. Remove with a slotted spoon, and drain well on paper toweling.

When all the strips have been fried, prepare honey glaze by combining the ½ cup sugar and the honey in a small saucepan. Cook and stir to boiling. (Watch carefully; honey scorches easily.) Continue cooking to hard ball stage (255°) or when a drop forms a hard ball in cold water. Stir in vanilla and cinnamon. On well-greased baking sheet, drizzle half the glaze over strips, tossing them to coat on all sides. With moistened hands, shape strips quickly into round log, 10 inches long and 3 inches wide. Drizzle remaining glaze over top and sides of log. Slice thinly to serve. Makes a 10-inch log.

Merry Christmas from Portugal

Ever since sixteenth-century explorers unlocked the →
spice chest of the Indies, cinnamon has scented Noel desserts such as Sonhos, fried cream puffs, Rabanados, fried ladyfingers, and a Nogados log.

Swedish Toasted Almond Cake

    3 tablespoons butter, melted
    ¼ cup graham cracker crumbs
    ¾ cup milk, scalded
    1½ cups sifted all-purpose flour
    2 teaspoons baking powder
    1 teaspoon salt
    3 eggs
    1½ cups sugar
    1 teaspoon vanilla
       Topping

Preheat electric skillet at 425°. Combine *1 table-spoon* butter and crumbs; coat bottom and sides of 9x9x2-inch baking pan. Pour remaining melted butter into milk. Sift together flour, baking powder, and salt. Beat eggs till thick and foamy. Gradually add sugar; continue beating till thick and lemon-colored. (Do not underbeat.) Add vanilla. Fold in flour mixture; stir in milk mixture. Pour into baking pan. Place on low rack in skillet. Bake, covered, for 65 to 70 minutes. Gently spread Topping around the outer edges of cake; bake, covered, 10 minutes. Serve warm or cold. Serves 10 to 12.

  Topping: In small skillet melt ⅓ cup butter or margarine. Add ¾ cup sliced almonds. Cook over low heat till lightly browned. Combine ⅓ cup sugar and 3 tablespoons all-purpose flour; add 2 tablespoons light cream. Stir into almond mixture; cook and stir till bubbly.

Skillet Cobbler

    2 cups packaged biscuit mix
    ¼ cup butter or margarine
    ¼ teaspoon ground cinnamon
    1 21-ounce can cherry pie filling
    ½ cup grated natural Cheddar cheese
       Cream or milk

Prepare biscuit mix according to package directions for biscuits. Roll ½ inch thick, and cut six 3-inch circles. Melt butter in electric skillet at 250°; add biscuits, turning once to coat both sides. Cover; close vent. Bake till browned, about 15 minutes. Turn and bake, covered, 2 or 3 minutes more. Stir ⅓ cup water and cinnamon into pie filling; spoon around biscuits. Sprinkle with cheese. Cover and heat through, 4 or 5 minutes. Serve with cream. Makes 6 servings.

Mocha Brownie Pudding

    1½ cups sifted all-purpose flour
    1¼ cups granulated sugar
    3 tablespoons unsweetened cocoa powder
    1 tablespoon baking powder
    1 tablespoon instant coffee powder
    ¾ teaspoon salt
    ¾ teaspoon ground ginger
    ¾ cup milk
    3 tablespoons cooking oil
    1½ teaspoons vanilla
    1 cup chopped walnuts
    1 cup brown sugar
    ⅓ cup unsweetened cocoa powder
    2½ cups hot water
       Vanilla ice cream
       Shredded orange peel (optional)

Sift together first 7 ingredients. Add milk, oil, and vanilla; mix till smooth. Stir in nuts. Spread evenly in greased 12-inch electric skillet. Combine the brown sugar, ⅓ cup cocoa, and hot water; pour over batter. Set heat control at 325°. Cover and bake, vent closed, till cake springs back when touched gently, 12 to 15 minutes. Spoon into serving dishes immediately. Top with ice cream and orange peel. Serves 8.

Steamed Chocolate Custard

    ½ cup semisweet chocolate pieces
    2 cups milk, scalded
    3 beaten eggs
    ⅓ cup sugar
    1 teaspoon vanilla
    ⅛ teaspoon salt
       Whipped cream or dessert topping
       Ground cinnamon

In a small skillet melt chocolate over low heat; gradually stir into milk. Cool slightly. In mixing bowl combine eggs, sugar, vanilla, and salt. Gradually stir in chocolate mixture. Pour into six 6-ounce custard cups. Set on rack in electric skillet; set heat control at 250°. Pour hot water into skillet to depth of ¾ inch. Cover, leaving vent open, and steam till knife inserted just off-center comes out clean, about 12 to 15 minutes. Serve warm or chilled in sherbet dishes; garnish with whipped cream and a dash of cinnamon. Makes 6 servings.

Caramel Floating Island

Pictured on page 64 —

> 5 eggs
> ⅓ cup sugar
> 3 cups milk
> ¾ cup sugar
> 1½ teaspoons vanilla

Separate *3 eggs;* beat whites till soft peaks form. Gradually add the ⅓ cup sugar, beating till stiff peaks form. In 10-inch skillet heat milk to simmering. Drop meringue in 8 portions into milk; simmer, uncovered, till firm, about 5 minutes. Lift from milk (reserve milk for custard); drain on paper toweling. Chill.

Slightly beat egg yolks with remaining 2 eggs; add ½ *cup* sugar and dash salt. Stir into reserved, slightly cooled milk. Cook and stir over low heat till mixture coats a metal spoon. Remove from heat; cool quickly in ice water. Add vanilla. Turn into serving bowl; chill. Top with meringues. Melt the remaining ¼ cup sugar in small heavy skillet over low heat, stirring constantly, till golden brown. Remove from heat. Immediately drizzle syrup over meringues in a thin, threadlike pattern. Makes 8 servings.

Toasted Almond Sponge

> 1 envelope unflavored gelatin
> ¾ cup sugar
> 1¼ cups milk, scalded
> ¼ cup sugar
> ½ teaspoon salt
> 1 teaspoon vanilla
> 1 cup whipping cream
> ½ cup toasted slivered almonds

Soften gelatin in ½ cup cold water. In heavy skillet caramelize ¾ cup sugar, stirring constantly so it doesn't burn. Remove from heat when a deep golden brown. Slowly add milk. Cook and stir till all caramel dissolves. Remove from heat. Add softened gelatin, the ¼ cup sugar, and salt; stir till dissolved. Add vanilla. Pour into bowl and chill till thick and syrupy. Whip cream; fold into gelatin. Fold in almonds, reserving a few for garnish. Chill till firm, 2 to 3 hours. Spoon into sherbet dishes. Top with reserved almonds. Serves 8 to 10.

Steamed Pumpkin Pudding

Pudding:
> ½ cup shortening
> 1 cup brown sugar
> ¼ cup granulated sugar
> ½ teaspoon ground cinnamon
> ½ teaspoon ground ginger
> ½ teaspoon ground nutmeg
> 2 eggs
>   • • •
> 2 cups sifted all-purpose flour
> 1½ teaspoons baking powder
> 1½ teaspoons salt
> ¼ teaspoon baking soda
> 1 cup canned pumpkin
> ½ cup dairy sour cream
> 1 cup chopped walnuts

Whipped Cream Sauce:
> 1 egg
> ¼ cup butter or margarine, melted
>   and cooled
> ¾ cup sifted powdered sugar
> ½ teaspoon vanilla
> ½ cup whipping cream

Pudding: In mixing bowl cream together shortening, brown and granulated sugars, and spices. Beat in 2 eggs. Sift together flour, baking powder, salt, and soda. Combine pumpkin and sour cream; add to creamed mixture alternately with sifted dry ingredients, mixing well after each addition. Fold in nuts.

Spoon pudding mixture into greased and floured 8-cup fancy ring mold; cover tightly with foil. Place in electric skillet at least 3 inches deep; pour in water to depth of 1 inch. Bring to boiling; reduce heat and set temperature control to simmer (250°). Cover and steam with vent closed 1¼ to 1½ hours. (If not using an electric skillet, set mold on a rack and fill pan with boiling water halfway up the mold; cover tightly and steam for 2 hours.) Remove mold and let stand for 10 minutes before unmolding. Serve warm with Whipped Cream Sauce. Garnish pudding with additional walnut halves, if desired.

Whipped Cream Sauce: In mixing bowl beat 1 egg till light and fluffy; gradually beat in butter, powdered sugar, vanilla, and dash salt. Whip cream. Gently fold whipped cream into egg mixture. Makes 1⅔ cups sauce.

Two-Tone Fudge

4½ cups sugar
1 14½-ounce can evaporated
   milk (1⅔ cups)
½ teaspoon salt

• • •

3 6-ounce packages semisweet chocolate
   pieces (3 cups)
2 4-ounce milk chocolate candy bars,
   broken in small pieces

• • •

1 7-ounce jar marshmallow creme
1 cup broken walnuts
1 teaspoon vanilla

In buttered, large, heavy skillet combine sugar, milk, and salt; bring to boiling. (Electric skillet 275°.) Cook and stir over medium heat to thread stage (candy thermometer 230°) or till syrup dropped from spoon spins a 2-inch thread. Remove from heat.

Working quickly, pour *half* (2 cups) of the mixture over semisweet chocolate pieces in a bowl, stirring till chocolate is melted. Pat in a buttered 15½x10½x1-inch pan.

Add the broken pieces of chocolate candy to the remaining cooked evaporated milk mixture; blend till smooth. Stir in marshmallow creme, nuts, and vanilla. Spread over first layer in pan. Chill till firm, at least 1 hour. Makes 5 pounds.

A heavy skillet keeps Buttery Peanut Brittle *from burning while it cooks to hard-crack stage (305°). A pinch of soda makes it porous enough to bite into.*

Energy Bars

2 tablespoons butter or margarine
2 cups miniature marshmallows or 20
   large marshmallows, snipped
2 tablespoons peanut butter
4 cups high-protein cereal

In heavy skillet melt butter. (Electric skillet 300°.) Add marshmallows; heat and stir till mixture is melted and syrupy. Remove from heat; stir in peanut butter. Add cereal and mix till coated. Press into an 8x8x2-inch square on a sheet of heavy foil. Cool till firm enough to cut into 2x1-inch bars. Makes 32.

Choco-Peanut Butter Squares

2 cups sugar
¾ cup peanut butter
1 6-ounce can evaporated milk
1 4½-ounce package instant chocolate
   pudding mix
2 cups quick-cooking rolled oats

In 10-inch skillet combine sugar, peanut butter, and milk. (Electric skillet 250°.) Over low heat, bring to slow boil, stirring till peanut butter is melted and sugar dissolves. Remove from heat. Add pudding mix and oats; mix thoroughly. Turn into 8x8x2-inch pan. Cool thoroughly. Cut into 1-inch squares. Makes 64.

Buttery Peanut Brittle

2 cups sugar
1 cup light corn syrup
1 cup butter or margarine
2 cups peanuts, skins removed
1 teaspoon baking soda

Heat and stir sugar, syrup, and ½ cup water in large, heavy skillet till sugar dissolves. (Electric skillet 250°.) When syrup boils, blend in butter. Stir often after 230° on candy thermometer; add nuts at 280°. Stir constantly to hard-crack stage (305°). Remove from heat. Quickly stir in soda, mixing well. Pour onto heavy foil. Stretch thin by lifting and pulling from edges with forks. Loosen from foil as soon as possible. Break up. Makes 2½ pounds.

Date-Nut Slices

    20 graham crackers
     2 tablespoons butter or margarine
     1 cup snipped pitted dates
     2 eggs
     1 cup sugar
     1 teaspoon vanilla
     1 cup flaked coconut
     ½ cup chopped walnuts

Crush graham crackers (2½ cups); set aside. Melt butter in medium skillet. (Electric skillet 300°.) Add dates and stir. Beat eggs and sugar together. Add to dates. Cook over low heat, stirring constantly, till sugar melts and mixture is thickened and bubbly, about 10 to 15 minutes.

   Remove from heat. Stir in vanilla; then stir in *2 cups* graham cracker crumbs, flaked coconut, and nuts. Cool to room temperature. Shape into four 7-inch rolls. Roll in the remaining ½ cup cracker crumbs, *or* 1 cup flaked coconut, *or* 1 cup chopped walnuts, if desired. Wrap in foil. Chill well. Slice thinly. Makes 72.

Candied Tangerine Peel

Give in brandy snifters as gifts to friends—

     8 medium tangerines or 6 oranges
     1 tablespoon salt
     4 cups cold water
     2 cups sugar
     ½ cup water

Cut peel of each tangerine into sixths; loosen from fruit with bowl of spoon. (If oranges are used, remove most of white membrane from peel.) Add salt to the 4 cups water; add peel. Weight with a plate to keep peel under water. Let stand overnight. Drain peel; wash thoroughly. Add enough cold water to cover; heat to boiling. Drain. Repeat 3 times. (This removes any bitter taste.) With kitchen shears, cut peel into triangular pieces or strips.

   In heavy skillet combine the cut peel (about 2 cups), the sugar, and the ½ cup water. (Electric skillet 275°.) Cook and stir till sugar dissolves. Cook slowly till peel is translucent. Drain thoroughly; coat with additional sugar. Dry on rack. Store in tightly covered container. Makes 2 to 2½ cups candied peel.

Sesame-Honey Candy

     2 cups sugar
     ⅔ cup honey
     ½ teaspoon ground ginger
     ⅔ cup chopped walnuts
     ½ cup sesame seed, toasted

In heavy skillet combine sugar, honey, ginger, and dash salt. Cook and stir over low heat till mixture boils; cook 8 minutes more, stirring occasionally. Remove from heat. Stir in nuts and sesame seed; pour onto greased platter. Cool slightly. Butter hands; press and spread candy very thin. Working quickly, cut into diamond-shaped pieces with shears while warm. (Candy will cool quickly.) Makes 6 dozen.

Quick Almond Brittle

     3 cups sugar
     ½ cup butter or margarine
       Dash salt
     1 cup chopped almonds
     1 6-ounce package semisweet chocolate
       pieces (1 cup)

Place sugar, butter, and salt in electric skillet at 400°. When sugar begins to melt, stir to blend. Cook and stir till sugar dissolves and color is a light golden brown, about 5 minutes. Turn control to 'off'; stir in ½ *cup* chopped almonds. Pour into buttered 15½x10½x1-inch pan. Cool. Melt chocolate over very low heat, stirring constantly. Spread over hardened candy. Sprinkle with remaining almonds. Break into pieces when cool. Makes about 2 pounds.

Orange-Coconut Brittle

Butter sides of large, heavy skillet or electric skillet. In it combine 2½ cups sugar, ¼ cup light corn syrup, 1 teaspoon shredded orange peel, and ½ cup orange juice. Cook over medium heat to hard-crack stage (candy thermometer 300°), stirring occasionally. Remove from heat; stir in 2 tablespoons butter. Pour a thin layer into buttered 15½x10½x1-inch pan. Sprinkle one 3½-ounce can flaked coconut (1⅓ cups) evenly over candy in pan. When cold, crack the candy. Makes 1¼ pounds.

Keep your skillets handy when preparing company meals. Many of these versatile pieces of cooking equipment are attractive enough to use when carrying food to the table. Others, such as the blazer pan of a chafing dish, a buffet-style electric frypan, or a Chinese wok, take you out of the kitchen by letting you do a little showmanship cookery in front of your guests.

Main dishes in this chapter center around meal plans for a variety of serving occasions. They include brunches, luncheons, dinners, and potlucks. Choose the entrée that best suits your own party plans and serve it with the other foods suggested. Then, the next time you are entertaining, follow the same basic plan, but substitute one of the other main course recipes suggested.

When the French serve pepper steak— *Steak au Poivre*—they rub the meat with freshly cracked peppercorns and cook it in brandy. You can make it from the recipe on page 90.

SUNDAY BRUNCH

Prepare one recipe from this page:

*Frittata Milanese with
Canadian-Style Bacon*

or

Ham Patties Hollandaise

Serve with:

*Crescent Rolls
Champagne Strawberries
Coffee*

Ham Patties Hollandaise

2 cups ground, fully cooked ham
½ cup long grain rice, cooked (1½ cups)
¼ cup chopped celery
2 tablespoons chopped onion
1 tablespoon chopped green pepper
¼ cup cooking oil
2 tablespoons all-purpose flour
1 teaspoon dry mustard
½ cup tomato juice

• • •

1 beaten egg
½ cup fine dry bread crumbs
Easy Hollandaise Sauce

Combine ground ham and rice. Cook celery, onion, and green pepper in 2 *tablespoons* oil till tender but not brown. Blend flour, dry mustard, and a dash pepper into vegetable mixture; add tomato juice. Cook and stir till very thick and bubbly. Add to ham mixture, mixing well; chill. Combine beaten egg and 1 tablespoon water. Form ham mixture into 8 patties; dip in egg mixture, then in bread crumbs.

In skillet cook patties in the remaining oil over medium heat till browned, 3 or 4 minutes on each side. (Electric skillet 300°.) Serve with Easy Hollandaise Sauce. Serves 4.

Easy Hollandaise Sauce: Prepare one ¾-ounce package hollandaise sauce mix according to package directions; combine the sauce with ¼ cup dairy sour cream. Heat and stir over low heat. (*Do not boil.*)

Frittata Milanese (Italian Omelet)

2 tablespoons chopped green onion
** with tops**
1 small clove garlic, minced
2 tablespoons butter or margarine

• • •

1 small zucchini, diced
1 medium tomato, peeled, chopped,
** and well drained**

• • •

6 eggs
¼ cup grated Parmesan cheese
1 tablespoon snipped parsley
¼ teaspoon salt
Freshly ground pepper

In an 8-inch oven-going skillet with nonstick finish, cook onion and garlic in butter till tender. In saucepan, cook zucchini in salted water till almost tender, about 5 minutes; drain. Add with tomato to onion and garlic; continue cooking till tomato is tender. Beat eggs till blended but not foamy. Add Parmesan cheese, parsley, salt, and pepper. Pour egg mixture over vegetables. Cook over low heat, without stirring, till set about ¼ inch around outer edge.

With a wide spatula, lift some of egg mixture from the sides of skillet, all the way around, tipping pan to let uncooked egg mixture flow to bottom. Continue cooking till top of frittata is *almost* set. Place skillet in 400° oven. Bake, uncovered, till top is set, 4 to 5 minutes. Loosen edges and invert onto serving dish. Cut in wedges. Makes 4 to 6 servings.

Canadian-Style Bacon

To panbroil, slash edges of ¼-inch-thick Canadian-style bacon slices. Preheat electric skillet to 350°. Brush lightly with cooking oil. Brown the bacon quickly, 2 or 3 minutes per side. One pound will make 6 servings.

Italian omelet for brunch

Frittata Milanese *goes well with* Canadian-Style → Bacon, *crescent rolls, and* Champagne Strawberries. *Marinate fresh strawberries in a little sugar and white wine. At serving time, add the chilled champagne.*

LUNCH'N OR BRUNCH'N

Prepare Swedish Pancakes and fill with:

Mushroom Sauce

or

Shrimp in Hollandaise Sauce

Serve with:

Fresh Asparagus and Lemon Butter

Mashed Potatoes

Fresh Fruits of the Season

Coffee

Shrimp in Hollandaise Sauce

4 egg yolks
6 tablespoons butter or margarine, softened
⅓ cup boiling water
1 tablespoon lemon juice
1 teaspoon dried dillweed
¾ teaspoon salt
1½ cups chopped, cleaned, cooked shrimp
• • •
12 Swedish Pancakes
• • •
2 tablespoons grated Parmesan cheese
1 teaspoon paprika
2 tablespoons butter or margarine

Cream egg yolks and 6 tablespoons butter in top of double boiler; stir in boiling water and cook over gently boiling water till thick and smooth, stirring constantly. Remove from heat and stir in lemon juice, dillweed, salt, and shrimp. Put 1 rounded tablespoon shrimp filling on unbrowned side of each pancake; roll up and place in 9x9x2-inch baking pan. Sprinkle with Parmesan and paprika; dot with butter.*

Cover and preheat electric skillet to 350° with vent closed. Place baking pan on rack; cover skillet and bake pancakes till heated through, about 30 minutes. Serves 4 to 6.

*Pancakes may be filled, covered with foil, and refrigerated till 45 minutes before serving time. Heat as above for the 45 minutes.

Mushroom Sauce

½ pound fresh mushrooms, sliced
2 tablespoons butter or margarine
2 tablespoons all-purpose flour
¾ teaspoon salt
1 cup light cream
1 tablespoon dry sherry
2 teaspoons lemon juice
• • •
12 Swedish Pancakes
2 tablespoons grated Parmesan cheese
1 teaspoon paprika
2 tablespoons butter or margarine

In skillet cook mushrooms in butter till tender, about 5 minutes. Stir in flour and salt. Add cream all at once. Cook quickly, stirring constantly, till mixture is thick and bubbly. Remove from heat; stir in dry sherry and lemon juice. Spoon 1 rounded tablespoon onto unbrowned side of each pancake, and roll up. Place rolled pancakes in 9x9x2-inch baking pan. Sprinkle with grated Parmesan cheese and paprika; dot with remaining butter.*

Cover and preheat electric skillet to 350° with vent closed. Place baking pan on rack; cover skillet and bake pancakes till heated through, about 30 minutes. Serves 4 to 6.

Swedish Pancakes

An electric skillet is ideal for baking these pancakes because it has even, controlled heat, and because its size permits baking more than one at a time—

2 eggs
1 cup milk
½ cup sifted all-purpose flour
2 teaspoons sugar
½ teaspoon salt

Combine all ingredients; beat with rotary beater till smooth. Bake in moderately hot, lightly greased electric skillet (375°), using 2 tablespoons batter for each pancake. Spread batter quickly and evenly to make thin cakes, 6 inches in diameter. When underside is light brown (about 1½ minutes), remove from skillet. Fill with Mushroom Sauce or Shrimp in Hollandaise Sauce, and bake as directed. Makes twelve 6-inch pancakes.

Spinach-Oyster Bisque

Puree one 8-ounce can oysters, drained, and ½ of 10-ounce package frozen spinach in blender. Heat 2 cups milk and 1 cup whipping cream to simmering in blazer pan of chafing dish. Stir in oyster purée, 2 tablespoons dry white wine, 2 tablespoons butter, ½ teaspoon salt, and ¼ teaspoon garlic salt. Simmer a few minutes. Keep warm over hot water bath. Trim with dairy sour cream. Makes 4 or 5 servings.

Creamed Sweetbreads on Toast

    1 pound sweetbreads
    1 tablespoon vinegar
    2 tablespoons butter or margarine
    3 tablespoons all-purpose flour
    ½ cup light cream
    1 tablespoon dry sherry or lemon juice
    8 to 12 toast points

Simmer sweetbreads in 1 quart water, ½ teaspoon salt, and the vinegar till tender, about 20 minutes. Drain, reserving ¾ cup stock. Cool sweetbreads; cube, carefully trimming away gristle and membrane present.

Melt butter in blazer pan of chafing dish; blend in flour, ½ teaspoon salt, and dash white pepper. Add reserved stock and cream. Cook, stirring constantly, till thickened and bubbly. Add sweetbreads and heat through, stirring gently. Stir in sherry. Keep warm over hot water (bain-marie). Serve over toast points. Serves 4.

Swedish Meatballs

Swedish women shape meatballs with a teaspoon measuring spoon. Dip spoon in cold water often, and chill the meatballs before browning—

    2 tablespoons butter or margarine
    1 tablespoon grated onion
    ½ pound ground veal
    ½ pound ground pork
    ½ cup light cream
    ¾ cup soft bread crumbs (1 slice)
    ¾ teaspoon salt
    ¼ teaspoon ground nutmeg
    ⅛ teaspoon white pepper
        • • •
    1 tablespoon all-purpose flour
    ¾ cup light cream

In heavy skillet melt butter; add onion and cook till golden but not brown. (Electric skillet 300°.) Combine meats, ½ cup cream, crumbs, salt, nutmeg, pepper, and onion, mixing till smooth. Wet hands; shape into 1-inch balls.

In same skillet brown the meatballs, shaking pan continuously to keep balls round (350°). Drain drippings into blazer pan of chafing dish. Stir in flour; blend in ¾ cup cream. Cook and stir till thickened and bubbly. Add meatballs. Cover and cook over low heat 15 minutes. Keep warm over hot water (bain-marie). Serves 6 to 8.

Brown the Swedish Meatballs in skillet, then prepare sauce in the blazer pan of chafing dish (also a skillet) to keep them warm during serving period.

CHINESE DINNER

Prepare one or more recipes from this page:

Sweet and Pungent Shrimp
Five-Spice Chicken
Tomato Beef

Serve with:

Chicken Broth or Egg Rolls (page 62)
Hot Cooked Rice
Lemon Sherbet and Almond Cookies
Tea

Tomato Beef

Basic gravy that glazes meat and vegetables is a mixture of cornstarch, oil, and soy sauce. Use the same mixture first to marinate the beef—

- 1½ **pounds boneless beef sirloin tip, cut in ½-inch thick slices**
- 1 **tablespoon cornstarch**
- 2 **tablespoons peanut or cooking oil**
- 3 **tablespoons soy sauce**
  Dash freshly ground pepper
  • • •
- ½ **teaspoon grated, fresh gingerroot or ½ teaspoon ground ginger**
- 1 **green pepper, sliced**
- ¼ **pound fresh mushrooms, sliced**
- 6 **green onions, cut in ½-inch pieces**
- 2 **small tomatoes, cut in wedges**

Partially freeze beef slices; cut diagonally in ¼-inch strips. Combine cornstarch, *1 table-spoon* oil, soy sauce, and pepper in bowl. Add beef; toss to coat well. Let stand several hours in refrigerator. Drain and save marinade.

Heat ginger in remaining tablespoon oil in electric wok or skillet at 350°. Add beef and stir-fry till brown, 5 to 6 minutes; push to one side. Add green pepper, mushrooms, and onions. Cook till tender-crisp, 2 or 3 minutes; push to one side. Add tomatoes; cover and cook 2 minutes. Pour reserved marinade over meat; cook and stir till thickened. Serves 4.

Sweet and Pungent Shrimp

- 1 **pound uncooked large shrimp in shells**
- 2 **beaten eggs**
- ½ **cup sifted all-purpose flour**
- 1½ **cups peanut or cooking oil**
- 2 **tablespoons cornstarch**
- ¾ **cup sugar**
- ¼ **cup vinegar**
  Dash freshly ground pepper
- ½ **cup canned pineapple chunks**
- 1 **large green pepper, cut in strips**
- 1 **tablespoon soy sauce**

Peel and clean shrimp, being careful to preserve tail shell; drain on paper toweling. Combine eggs, flour, ¾ teaspoon salt, and ¼ cup water; beat smooth. Heat oil in electric wok or skillet at 375°. Dip shrimp in batter. Add 5 or 6 shrimp at a time to oil; cook till golden brown, about 5 minutes. Drain on paper toweling. In saucepan blend cornstarch with ¾ cup cold water. Add sugar, vinegar, and pepper. Cook and stir till thickened and bubbly. Add pineapple, green pepper, and soy sauce. Heat 1 or 2 minutes more. Serve with shrimp. Serves 4.

Five-Spice Chicken

Combine 1 teaspoon *each* ground cinnamon and crushed aniseed, ½ teaspoon salt, ¼ teaspoon ground allspice, and ⅛ teaspoon *each* ground cloves and freshly ground pepper. Rub 4 chicken breasts with 1 *teaspoon* of the mixture. (Save remainder of mixture for another day.) Heat 2 tablespoons peanut or cooking oil and 1 clove garlic, crushed, in skillet. (Electric skillet 350°.) Add chicken; brown on both sides. Reduce heat (220°). Add ¾ cup unsweetened pineapple juice; simmer, covered, till chicken is tender, 35 minutes. Transfer chicken to platter; spoon sauce over. Garnish with parsley. Serves 4.

Take a wok

Use two woks if you're cooking Tomato Beef for more than four people. Push the browned meat and vegetables up the flared sides of the pans while remaining portions cook in the oil centered at the bottom.

MIDWEST POTLUCK SUPPER

Prepare one or more recipes from these pages:

Ham Loaves

Scalloped Potatoes and Ham

Jungle Hash

Chicken Lasagne

Pork Marengo

Porcupine Meatballs

Canadian-Smoked Limas

Serve with:

Coleslaw or Carrot-Pineapple Mold

Hot Buttered Cornbread Squares

Chocolate Cake

Scalloped Potatoes and Ham

      6 medium potatoes, peeled and sliced
      3 tablespoons butter or margarine
   ¾ cup soft bread crumbs (1 slice)
   ½ teaspoon paprika
   ⅛ teaspoon dried thyme leaves, crushed

          •   •   •

      2 tablespoons all-purpose flour
      1 teaspoon salt
      1 teaspoon dry mustard
      1 cup milk or light cream
      4 slices process American cheese, cut up
          (4 ounces)
      2 cups cubed fully cooked ham

Cook potatoes in boiling, salted water till tender, 10 to 15 minutes. Drain, reserving 1 cup cooking liquid. Place potatoes in 8x8x2-inch baking dish. Melt butter in skillet. (Electric skillet 300°.) Remove 1 tablespoon butter; toss with crumbs, paprika, and thyme. Set aside.

Into remaining butter in skillet, blend flour, salt, mustard, and ⅛ teaspoon pepper. Add milk and reserved liquid from potatoes; cook and stir till thickened and bubbly. Stir in cheese and ham; cook till cheese is melted. Pour over potatoes. Sprinkle with crumbs. Place on low rack in electric skillet. Cover and bake with vent open at 350° for 1 hour. Serves 6 to 8.

Chicken Lasagne

      1 16-ounce can tomatoes, cut up
      1 15-ounce can tomato sauce
      2 slices boiled ham, diced
      1 3-ounce can chopped mushrooms,
          drained
   ½ cup Marsala or dry red wine
      1 clove garlic, minced
      1 teaspoon dried rosemary leaves, crushed
   ½ teaspoon dried sage leaves, crushed
      1 bay leaf
      6 ounces lasagne noodles, cooked
   1½ cups diced mozzarella cheese (6 ounces)
   1½ cups freshly grated Romano cheese
   1½ cups cottage cheese or ricotta, drained
      2 cups diced, cooked chicken

In large skillet combine first 9 ingredients. (Electric skillet 250°.) Simmer, uncovered, till slightly thickened, 15 to 20 minutes. Remove bay leaf. Spoon a *third* of the sauce into a 9x9x2-inch baking pan. Place 3 or 4 lasagne noodles over it. Combine cheeses. Layer *half* the cheeses and chicken atop noodles. Spoon ⅓ more sauce over. Repeat layers of noodles, cheese, chicken, and sauce. Line electric skillet with heavy foil, or use low rack. Place pan on foil. Cover, leaving vent open. Bake at 350° for 45 minutes. Uncover; let stand 10 to 15 minutes before serving. Serves 6 to 8.

Jungle Hash

      3 slices bacon
      1 pound ground beef
   ¾ cup chopped celery
   ½ cup chopped onion
   ½ cup chopped green pepper
      1 teaspoon salt
      1 15-ounce can kidney beans, drained
   ⅓ cup uncooked long grain rice
   1½ cups water

In skillet cook bacon till crisp; crumble and set aside. (Electric skillet 350°.) Pour off drippings. In same skillet cook ground beef, celery, onion, and green pepper till meat is browned and vegetables are tender. Season with salt and dash pepper. Spoon off excess fat. Stir in remaining ingredients. Cover and reduce heat (220°). Simmer till rice is tender, about 30 minutes. Serves 4.

Pork Marengo

1¼ cups sliced, fresh mushrooms or
    1 3-ounce can sliced mushrooms,
    drained
2 tablespoons butter or margarine
2 pounds lean pork or veal, cut in ½-inch
    cubes
12 small pearl onions, peeled
4 medium tomatoes, quartered
½ cup dry white wine or chicken broth
1 teaspoon salt
1 teaspoon dried marjoram leaves,
    crushed
1 teaspoon dried thyme leaves, crushed

In heavy skillet cook mushrooms in butter for 2 minutes. (Electric skillet 250°.) Remove from skillet. Increase heat (300°); add pork and onions; brown well. Add tomatoes, wine, salt, marjoram, thyme, and dash pepper. Cover; reduce heat (220°). Simmer till pork is tender, about 1 hour. Tomato sauce should be thick; if not, remove meat and onions to platter and keep warm; turn up heat and cook sauce till desired consistency. Add mushrooms; heat through. Pour sauce over meat. Serves 6 to 8.

Canadian-Smoked Limas

1 10-ounce package frozen lima beans
½ cup dairy sour cream
2 teaspoons all-purpose flour
3 teaspoons brown sugar
1 teaspoon chicken-flavored gravy base
¾ teaspoon grated orange peel
3 tablespoons orange juice
1 tablespoon butter or margarine
6 slices Canadian-style bacon, cut
    in thin strips (6 ounces)

Cook limas according to package directions; drain well, reserving ¼ cup cooking liquid. Stir together reserved liquid, sour cream, flour, *1 teaspoon* brown sugar, gravy base, orange peel, and juice. In skillet melt butter. (Electric skillet 350°.) Add meat; brown lightly. Remove from skillet; toss with remaining brown sugar and keep warm. In same skillet combine limas and sour cream mixture. Heat and stir just to boiling. Turn onto serving platter. Arrange bacon strips over top. Makes 3 or 4 servings.

Porcupine Meatballs

1 beaten egg
1 tablespoon milk
½ cup day-old bread crumbs (¾ slice)
½ cup uncooked packaged precooked rice
¾ teaspoon salt
    Dash freshly ground pepper
1 pound ground beef
1 tablespoon butter or margarine
1 7½-ounce can tomatoes, cut up
1 cup hot water
1 sprig fresh basil or ½ teaspoon
    dried basil leaves, crushed

Combine egg, milk, crumbs, rice, salt, and pepper; add ground beef and mix well. Shape meat into about 20 small balls. In heavy skillet brown in hot butter on all sides, turning gently. (Electric skillet 350°.) Drain off excess fat. Add tomatoes, water, and basil. Cover and simmer until tender, about 45 minutes, turning once or twice. Makes 4 or 5 servings.

Ham Loaves

2 beaten eggs
1 cup saltine cracker crumbs
⅔ cup milk
    Dash freshly ground pepper
1 pound ground fully cooked ham
1 pound ground fresh pork
1 8¼-ounce can pineapple slices, drained
2 maraschino cherries, halved
½ cup brown sugar
1 teaspoon dry mustard
2 tablespoons vinegar

Combine eggs, cracker crumbs, milk, and pepper. Add meats; mix well. In 7½x3¾x2¼-inch loaf pan arrange 2 slices pineapple and 2 cherry halves in bottom. Firmly press *half* the meat mixture into pan. Loosen sides with spatula. Unmold into 9x9x2-inch baking pan. Repeat with remaining pineapple, cherries, and meat mixture, unmolding second loaf into same pan.

    Cover and preheat electric skillet to 375°. Place pan of meat loaves on low rack in skillet. Cover; bake with vent closed for 1 hour and 10 minutes. Drain off fat. Combine brown sugar, mustard, and vinegar; spoon over meat. Cover; bake 10 minutes more. Makes 8 servings.

CROSS-COUNTRY FAVORITES

Prepare one of the recipes from these pages:

Steak au Poivre
Steak with Lobster Tail
Wine-Sauced Hamburger Steak
Elegant Beef Tenderloin
Oriental-Stuffed Steaks

Serve with:

Baked Potatoes
Tomato Halves with Garden Peas
Bibb Lettuce/Artichoke Salad
Hot French Bread
Caramel Floating Island (page 77)

Steak au Poivre (French Pepper Steak)

Pictured on page 80—

- 2 to 4 teaspoons whole black peppercorns
- 4 beef top loin or strip steaks, cut 1 inch thick (2¼ pounds)
- ¼ cup butter or margarine
- ¼ cup chopped shallots or green onions
- 1 beef bouillon cube
- 3 tablespoons brandy

Coarsely crack peppercorns with mortar and pestle or in metal mixing bowl with bottom of a bottle. Place one steak on waxed paper. Sprinkle with ¼ to ½ teaspoon cracked peppercorns; rub over meat and press in with heel of hand. Turn steak and repeat. Continue with remaining steaks. In 12-inch skillet melt 2 *tablespoons* butter. (Electric skillet 325°.) Cook steaks over medium-high heat to desired doneness, 11 to 12 minutes for medium. Season with salt. Transfer to hot serving plate; keep hot.

Cook shallots in remaining 2 tablespoons butter till tender but not brown, about 1 minute. Add bouillon cube and ⅓ cup water; boil rapidly over high heat 1 minute, scraping up browned bits from pan. Add brandy; cook 1 minute more. Pour over steaks. Serves 4.

Steak with Lobster Tail

The Surf 'n Turf or Lob-Steer combination is a menu hit coast to coast. Can't decide between steak and seafood? Serve guests some of each.

- 4 beef top loin or strip steaks, cut 1 inch thick
- 4 4-ounce frozen lobster tails
- ¼ cup butter or margarine, melted
- 2 teaspoons lemon juice
- ¼ teaspoon salt
  Dash paprika

Slash fat edge of steaks at 1-inch intervals. In skillet brown the steaks, uncovered, over medium-high heat, turning occasionally, a total of 9 to 10 minutes for rare; 11 to 12 minutes for medium; or 20 minutes for well-done. (Electric skillet 350°.) Season with salt and pepper. Meanwhile, drop frozen lobster tails in boiling, salted water to cover. Bring to boiling; reduce heat and simmer 8 minutes. Drain. Snip along each side of the thin undershell and remove undershell. Remove lobster meat from shells and cut in chunks. Return meat to shells and place one atop each steak. Blend remaining ingredients; spoon over lobster. Makes 4 servings.

Elegant Beef Tenderloin

- 4 beef tenderloin steaks, cut ½ inch thick
- 1 tablespoon butter or margarine
- ¼ cup brandy
- ½ cup dairy sour cream
- 2 tablespoons catsup
- ¼ teaspoon salt
- 2 dashes Worcestershire sauce
- 2 drops bottled hot pepper sauce
  Dash ground thyme

In skillet brown the steaks in butter on both sides to desired doneness, 6 to 8 minutes for medium-rare. (Electric skillet 350°.) Remove from heat and spoon 2 *tablespoons* brandy over steaks. Place steaks on warm platter and keep hot while making sauce.

Combine sour cream, catsup, salt, Worcestershire, hot pepper sauce, thyme, and the remaining brandy; add to same skillet. Heat, stirring constantly, just till hot. Spoon some sauce over steaks; pass remainder. Makes 4 servings.

Serve Elegant Beef Tenderloin *with a sour cream sauce, tomato halves with garden peas, and tender asparagus. When you are watching your budget, substitute a less-costly cut such as a club or rib steak.*

Oriental-Stuffed Steak

4 beef T-bone steaks, cut ¾ inch
    thick (3 pounds)
½ of 6-ounce package long grain and
    wild rice mix
1 beaten egg
2 tablespoons sliced green onion
    with tops
¼ to ½ cup bottled teriyaki sauce

Using a sharp knife, carefully cut a pocket in largest muscle of each steak. Cook rice according to package directions. Cool slightly; stir in egg and onion. Stuff steaks with mixture, using about ⅓ cup for each. In 12-inch skillet panbroil steaks till desired doneness, about 4 to 6 minutes on each side for medium-rare. (Electric skillet 325°.) Brush often with teriyaki sauce. Makes 4 servings.

Wine-Sauced Hamburger Steak

¾ pound lean ground beef
½ teaspoon salt
    Dash pepper
1 tablespoon butter or margarine
2 tablespoons dry red wine
2 teaspoons dried parsley flakes
1 teaspoon lemon juice
½ teaspoon instant minced onion
¼ teaspoon Worcestershire sauce

Combine ground beef, salt, and pepper; mix well. Shape into 2 patties about ½ inch thick. In skillet brown the meat in butter over medium-high heat till medium-rare, about 2 minutes on each side. (Electric skillet 325°.) Remove to warm plates. Add wine, parsley flakes, lemon juice, onion, and Worcestershire sauce to skillet; heat to boiling. Pour over meat. Serves 2.

PORCH PARTY SUPPER

Prepare one of the recipes from this page:

Paella à la Valenciana
Ham with Vegetable Garland
Chicken Sevillano

Serve with:

Tossed Green Salad with Watercress
Pears and Bel Paese or Brie Cheese
Toasted Almond Sponge
(Recipe page 77)

Paella à la Valenciana

- ½ **pound pork shoulder, cubed**
- 1 **2- to 2½-pound ready-to-cook broiler-fryer chicken, cut up**
- ¼ **cup cooking oil**
- 1½ **teaspoons salt**
- 2 **cloves garlic, crushed**
- 1½ **cups uncooked long grain rice**
- 1 **large onion, chopped**
- 3 **cups chicken broth**
- ½ **teaspoon thread saffron, crushed**
- ¼ **teaspoon dried tarragon leaves, crushed**
- ¼ **teaspoon dried oregano leaves, crushed**
- 4 **tomatoes, quartered**
- 6 **clams in shells, washed**
- 8 **ounces fresh or frozen shelled shrimp**
- 1 **9-ounce package frozen artichoke hearts**

Brown the pork, then the chicken in hot oil in large skillet or paella pan. (Electric skillet 350°.) Sprinkle with *1 teaspoon* salt; add garlic. Reduce heat (300°). Cover and cook till both are tender, 30 minutes. Remove from skillet. Pour off all but 2 tablespoons drippings. Add rice and onion; cook till golden, stirring frequently. Combine next 4 ingredients and the remaining ½ teaspoon salt. Pour over rice. Cover and cook over low heat till rice is almost tender, 20 minutes. Add tomatoes, clams, shrimp, pork, chicken, and artichokes; cook 15 to 20 minutes longer. Makes 6 servings.

Ham with Vegetable Garland

- 1 **5- to 7-pound boneless fully cooked ham**
- 1 **small head cauliflower, broken into flowerettes (4 cups)**
- 6 **carrots, peeled and bias sliced**
- ½ **teaspoon dillweed**
- ⅛ **teaspoon pepper**
- ¼ **cup butter or margarine**
- 2 **9-ounce packages frozen Italian green beans**
- ¼ **cup orange marmalade**

Place ham, fat side up, on rack in electric skillet with a high dome cover. Score top of ham. Insert meat thermometer. Cover; bake at 350° till thermometer registers 130°, about 1½ to 2 hours. Place cauliflower and carrots around ham. Combine 1 cup water, 1 teaspoon salt, the dillweed, and pepper; pour over vegetables. Dot with butter. Cover and cook till vegetables are tender, about 35 minutes. Add beans; brush ham with marmalade. Cook 10 minutes more. Makes 8 to 10 servings.

Chicken Sevillano

- 3 **chicken breasts, skinned and split**
- 3 **tablespoons butter or margarine, melted**
- 1 **clove garlic, minced**
- 1 **pound potatoes, peeled and quartered**
- 1 **9-ounce package frozen artichoke hearts, thawed**
- ½ **cup pitted ripe olives, halved**
- ⅓ **cup dry sherry**
- ¾ **cup light cream**
- 2 **teaspoons all-purpose flour**

In large, heavy skillet brown the chicken in butter with garlic. (Electric skillet 350°.) Season with salt and pepper. Add potatoes. Cover and simmer 20 minutes. Reduce heat (220°); add artichoke hearts and olives. Continue cooking till potatoes are tender, about 10 minutes. Arrange chicken, potatoes, artichokes, and olives on platter; keep warm. Add sherry to skillet and scrape pan to remove drippings. Combine cream, flour, ¼ teaspoon salt, and ⅛ teaspoon pepper. Stir into sherry mixture; cook and stir till thick. Pour over chicken. Makes 6 servings.

INDEX

A-B

D-F